IT'S NOT ABOUT SELF-ESTEEM, SELF-WORTH IS THE KEY TO SUCCESS

Laila-Elizabeth Risdon

Lubabe Books

ISBN: 9798367379617

Cover design by Richard Thomas.
Headshot photo by Jo Welch Photography.
Escape Routes photo by Oliver Hurd Thomas.
All photos © Indigo Brave.
Graphics for The SELF Model™ by Heather Willey.
Edited by Rebecca Brittain and Lara-Mae Delmage.
Published by www.LuBaBeBooks.co.uk.

To Mathew, Luke and Esmée, my greatest teachers.

And to all my true friends and family. Thank you for being there. For sticking with me. You're the reason I have been able to get back up again... and again... and again. In gratitude and awe.

Lastly, I dedicate this book to all our clients! Thank you so much for your trust, courage, and your willingness to grow. You have all given of yourselves and contributed to our growth since 1996. I am hugely grateful and appreciate everything you have given to me and Indigo Brave.

"I'm a contributor, not a guru."

DENISE DUFFIELD THOMAS

ACKNOWLEDGMENT

I would like to acknowledge that I did not start Indigo Brave alone. However, some of the early members of Indigo Brave wished to stay anonymous, and others could not be contacted. Therefore, I will simply refer to Indigo Brave as 'we' throughout the book. I am so grateful to the founders, members, trustees, champions, and employees of Indigo Brave. You were instrumental to the spirit and the creation of the company which we have today. I also want to thank and acknowledge the current team, who are a truly exceptional group of people and a hugely positive force in the world.

Names have been changed where appropriate.

PRAISE FOR THE AUTHOR

"Laila helped me create a life I never felt worthy of having."
Nekita.

"I have got more out of your coaching in six months than in a lifetime of working on these issues." Operations Manager, Blue Chip Company.

"My confidence has soared; I've changed how I interact with the world." Dr Kim Kenobi.

"You are hands down one of the best people I've ever met. Your coaching has been a total inspiration to me. Thanks for sharing your model, which has been revelatory to me, and bits of your story." Dr Sophie Parker-Norman, Head of R&D.

"Words can't truly describe the impact seeing Laila intermittently for over a decade has had, both personally and professionally. Working in a similar field perhaps

makes me harder to please, but the combination of Laila's knowledge, wisdom and warmth has worked. I am far more fulfilled, happier and have a significantly better understanding of myself, and my interactions with others, as a result of her coaching." Consultant Psychiatrist, UK.

"Laila has taught me so much about the conflicts I was facing, I'm now a lot braver about having difficult conversations in my personal and professional life. I am reaping the benefits and it's gold!" Melanie Womack, Commercial Director

"Laila taught me how to be an authentic leader. I learned to harness my personal strengths in order to deliver more effectively and efficiently, in my own style too! It moved my team from 'great' to 'outstanding'. Within nine months of working with Laila my serious skin complaint was gone and I negotiated a pay rise and directorship too!" Johann Smith, Product Development Director.

"Working with Laila has been transformational and profoundly life changing...why? Increased self-awareness, understanding others and increased decision-making ability, recognising choices where previously I could see none. It has overflowed powerfully into my home life. It has sometimes been tough, but 100% worth it." Ian Hemstock, Operations Director.

THE PREMISE OF THIS BOOK

"The simplest solution is almost always the best." Occam's Razor

This book will change how you think about yourself forever. Through years of working with humans in all their complexity – a simple model has been born and it's changing lives.

It's called: The SELF Model™

The SELF Model™ teaches the key differences between self-confidence, self-esteem and self-worth. This model has helped tens of thousands of people over the years since I had the good fortune to stumble upon it. It provides a way of understanding a crucial aspect of how we view ourselves; how we interpret our inner world and what that means to our interaction with the outer world. It supports us to get really clear on the language we use to identify who we are, what we do and ultimately what it means to be human.

From this book, you will learn that your worth as a human is not the same as your self-esteem. You will find out that your self-esteem will not, and should not, be good all the time. You will learn that self-esteem should in fact fluctuate, and this is normal. You will learn that your self-worth on the other hand, should not fluctuate; it should be unassailable.

You have worth simply because you are human; you are a unique, amazing collection of biological cells, that we are still at the beginning of understanding, and which, when all put together, make you a living, breathing being. No matter what your worldview is, whether you believe in a creator or not, you are part of this universe and you have worth simply because you exist. There is nothing that you could ever do, good or bad, that can take away from that.

This is not a theory book and I am definitely not an academic. This model came out of real-life experiences, and I have seen it make such a change to so many people, it simply has to be shared as widely as possible. There is no right way to read this book, it depends on how you will best make sense of this new information to integrate it into your life. It is an experiential book, designed to support you to change the way you understand yourself, forever.

The second half of this book explains the model and is a practical approach to a deep understanding of how to build success in your life by building real resilience and appropriate self-confidence – all of which can only be done if you are able to truly understand the key difference between your self-worth and self-esteem. Understanding is only the first step of course, so there are some real-life stories and plenty of tried and tested techniques which will support you to develop abilities to own your self-worth and crucially how to ensure it is separated from your self-esteem. This will help you to integrate the fundamentals of this model into your life and feel better in your skin.

The visual graphics of The SELF Model™ are in Part 2 of the book and if you like to learn visually, you may want to go straight there and make sense of it that way. Or perhaps you would like to understand where it came from first, in which case, you might like to have a wander with me, while I share how we discovered how powerful this model is and why we know it really works.

INTRODUCTION

In western culture we have become far too focused on developing and maintaining good self-esteem. We preach that everyone can do everything and anyone can achieve anything; everyone can get an A** and that is what good education is about. We remove competitions in case losing affects the self-esteem of children who don't win. We focus on self-esteem and consciously try to improve it, and yet all mental health issues are increasing in young adults and in our young people; the same young people who have had the most deliberate input in terms of building good self-esteem. I'm sure you know from your friends and family that young people are suffering with more anxiety, depression, low mood etc. The figures on mental health in young people are alarming. Medical conditions like depression are on the rise, self-harm is rising, even suicide is rising.

The Good Childhood Report 2022 from The Children's Society shows that children's happiness continues to decline. Five children in a classroom of 30 are likely to have a mental health problem. The group most at risk are young women aged 17 to 22 with 52% of 17- to 23-year-olds experiencing mental health deterioration in the last five years. 50% of mental health issues begin before the age of 14.* The COVID pandemic has clearly had an effect on these figures, but the trend started well before then.

*Source: Children's Mental Health Statistics | The Children's Society.

The call for Self-Love is certainly on the rise. But is that the answer? It doesn't seem to really get to the heart of the matter. I see people getting up early to do 'an hour of ME time' before the day starts. Self-care is a whole industry and this Valentine's Day (February 2023) Flowers, the single by Miley Cyrus, was at No 1 "I can buy myself flowers… I can love myself."

But all too often I witness that positive idea turn into yet another 'To Do' job! Another drive in our attempt to push ourselves into becoming better. The 5am club has often turned insomnia into a 'must have'. It is hard to go to bed at 9pm each night and we definitely do know that lack of sleep has been proven to be detrimental for your health.

More To Do lists, more goals and more inevitable failure when you don't manage to keep getting up at 5am to 'love yourself better'! More loving yourself because – at last – now you are going to be able to become… thinner, bendier, healthier, more well read, more zen after your hour's meditation (fill in the gap for yourself…).

But this person, the one who needs to achieve these goals, will never be satisfied by them. You are not defined by them. This is not you. It is merely what you can do. If you turn loving yourself into another set of targets and activities, it will lead to stress, pressure, achievement-driven 'tick box' exercises – all of which are fine in the right place, but none of which can, or ever will, improve your actual levels of self-love. It can't. It is in the wrong place. It may even lead you to need to DO more in order to create the image of yourself that you think is OK. And that can lead you to actually be loving that 'image' of yourself. That is not self-love. There's a different name for that.

Narcissism is certainly on the rise. In the general population and in our leaders. We must understand more about this complicated personality trait and disorder but let's dispel a simple myth now. People often think that narcissism is about 'loving yourself' but it's not. Narcissus did not fall in love with himself. He fell in love with the reflection of himself. When we are praised and appreciated for the projection of ourselves, without self-worth underneath it, we can start to believe that is us, and perhaps even fall in love with a 'show reel' life, and that can lead to a very empty life indeed.

Surely all the modern focus on 'me time' and 'self-love' is a great thing? Surely as we all learn to love and accept ourselves, to believe in ourselves to a greater degree, then we should be improving? Living healthier, happier, more fulfilled lives?

So Why Doesn't It Work?

Please understand I am not in any way against ambition, achievement or working hard to become the best version of ourselves. Neither am I against encouragement, acknowledgment or praise. But clearly something we are doing is wrong because it simply isn't working.

The concept of self-esteem as a necessary skill for life seems to have taken hold in California in the 1980s. It was proposed that building self-esteem would be some kind of silver bullet, supporting the healthy development of young people, lowering crime rates, drug addiction, unemployment, the works. Will Storr investigated this in depth in his book, *Selfie: How we became so self-obsessed and what it's doing to us.* (Pan Macmillan 2017)

Although the California experiment gained much positive press at the time, this turned out to be a carefully constructed PR campaign, which seems to have focused solely on the narrative of the project, ignoring all the data. The data from the University of California concluded that "the association between self-esteem and its expected consequences are mixed, insignificant or absent" (from Storr's Guardian Article 2017).

However, the urban myth had taken hold and more than 30 years later the idea that self-esteem is good, and needs to be built and protected, is still a defining idea of most of our education and workplace establishments.

I believe that the task force did not achieve their intended result because they focused on self-esteem without actually understanding what that was. They took a dictionary definition of self-esteem and believed it to be synonymous with self-worth. My experience would suggest that had they understood how different these two aspects of our self-regard are, then their results would have been very different.

MY CAMPAIGN TO CHANGE THE DICTIONARY DEFINITION

Dear Oxford English Dictionary,

I write regarding your definition of self-worth:

> *Self-worth (noun) a feeling of confidence in yourself that you are a good and useful person. synonym: self-esteem.*

I would like to request a re-definition. I respectfully ask that when people pick up the Oxford English Dictionary, they discover that their self-worth is who they are; their qualities, their uniqueness, their human being-ness. My 25 years of research with over 20,000 people, mainly, but not exclusively, in the UK, has proved that self-esteem and self-worth are not synonyms. They are not interchangeable.

My suggestion is for a redefinition of both terms:

Self-esteem (noun); how we feel about what we can do, our achievements, our abilities, our 'doings' in the world.

Self-worth (noun); your intrinsic, immutable, inarguable worth as a human being. Your 'BE'ING-ness.

I look forward to hearing from you.

Kind Regards,

Laila-Elizabeth Risdon

Why Am I Writing To The Oxford English Dictionary?

I believe that we are constantly shifting our understanding of what it is to be a human being and how to live up to our potential on this planet.

Our language must reflect this, as it is one of our main ways of communicating. Therefore, I am asking for this simple but profound shift from the 'guardians' of the English language.

That our worth is not dependent on our ability to 'do'.

Looking into the etymology of 'worth' I discover that the word comes from Middle English and Germanic roots and means worthy, valuable. Interestingly, as a suffix -worth means 'enclosed place, homestead'.

'Esteem' comes from the Latin verb meaning to value. And here we find a paradox. Just because we know something is VALUABLE, it doesn't mean we can give it 'A VALUE' we can't reduce humanness to a 'more or less' value. I am valuable – this does not mean I have a value that is more or less than someone else's. I am a human being, not a human doing. (I also think it is dangerous to reduce the idea of human beings to a 'resource' but that is probably for another day!)

Self-worth is not what you can do, make, create, achieve, own, have etc. Your intrinsic worth is not debatable. It just is. The OED advises that you should: 'Praise your child to increase her sense of self-worth.' This is wrong. It isn't only the OED that is wrong – it is every parent/caregiver who has praised a child for doing something 'clever' or 'well' without remembering to make sure that the child is not basing their sense of worth on that ability. At one time or another, every person has DONE something good and therefore, felt that because of that, that they ARE good.

Do you like a good TV comedy? In the search for evening entertainment with our teenagers, we have discovered a new world of comedy series that we can all enjoy as a family. Apart from some quality time laughing with our teens, it also gifted me with one of the best examples of the obvious issues of mixing up your esteem and worth.

Jake Peralta, a New York Detective in Brooklyn 99 repeats this pattern of behaviour many times in the show. He's connecting the dots and a good lead turns out to be correct. "I'm the greatest detective ever and I'm never going to die," he cries with effusive joy. Ten minutes later in the same episode, his lead goes cold, he is devastated and howls: "I'm a horrible person and I will die alone….". He has definitely mixed up his self-worth and his self-esteem. We may not all do this to the extent that Jake Peralta does – but we do it every time we let something we have done affect our sense of worth.

If we accept the OED definitions, then to have self-worth we must be praised for things we are DOING. Therefore, we must be GOOD at what we are DOING. But we are NOT always good at what we are doing, a lot of the time we are quite dreadful at what we are doing. We make mistakes, we misjudge situations, we make assumptions, we fail to communicate what we mean, we let our emotions rule our actions, we get upset, we act rashly.

Your worth is unassailable. It is not a 'thing' that is open to being measured on a scale designed by human beings. It is yours. Your worth. Unique, immeasurable, possibly indefinable, but yours. Most importantly, it is NOT your esteem. You don't have to do great things to be a great person, and you can't make yourself a great person by doing good things. Our doing is haphazard and inconsistent at best and irrational and criminal at worst. Motivations are complicated. Is a good action good if the motivation is not good? As our 'doing' becomes more and more complex and impactful, enhanced in its power by technologies and worldwide reach, I believe we need to better understand our 'doing' and make clear separation from our being.

Our worth is intrinsic and unassailable; however, we all know that we do not always live up to our worth in our actions, and that paradox is ultimately a very human thing. We need to become far more sophisticated in our ability to separate our worth from our esteem and not to confuse either of them with our 'value'.

In the English language, it's easy to confuse worth and value, but they are not the same at all. Your Worth is NOT your 'value' to other people, or to society. This 'value' of course can be deemed more or less if your actions are considered more, or less, 'beneficial' to society. But that is not your inner worth. Ultimately, only you can really know your own worth. Your inner world of you-ness. I hope this little book might start you on the journey of why you must separate your worth and esteem, and how to actually do it.

HOW THE SELF MODEL™ CAME INTO BEING

The Arts in Education movement in Nottingham in the mid-nineties was vibrant. Think orchestras, jazz bands, rock schools, drama sessions, dance schools and theatre shows. There was a real commitment to the Arts through a council-funded programme called the 11th Session. The 11th Session grew from the idea that in addition to the ten morning and afternoon sessions of the school week, there should be an 11th one: an extracurricular session of arts (music, any visual art, drama etc.) completely free and available for every young person. Everyone could choose a session if they wanted to, in whatever arts activity they wanted to have a go at. Bands, jazz, theatre, puppetry, dance; there was tuition available for just about any artistic activity you could think of.

Some of it was open access and have-a-go level, some of it was audition level and professional standard. The Young People's Theatre Company went to the Edinburgh Festival to perform each summer with musicals, contemporary dance pieces, commissioned music, plays and devised pieces with young people with special needs. I was a jobbing actor and musician at the time and these were very special opportunities for me. It wasn't only young people, there was a programme for adults too, and I got to work as part of a huge and ever shifting team of professional actors and musicians, tutors from RADA and visiting theatre companies from across the world. It was very inspiring. I accepted acting jobs and tours when they came along and got to work on a huge range of rewarding projects when I was back.

In 1995 I was invited to work on an Arts Council-commissioned half-day drama workshop designed to increase the aspirations of young women by exploring influential women's real-life stories. The project was called Women of Influence. It sought to build the confidence of young women and inspire them to reach their potential. I was teamed up with a group of fellow actresses and facilitators who shared my love of using drama and the arts for self-development.

The group of sulky, too-cool-for-school, young women strutted into the drama studio. They were not happy to be there and said things along the lines of: "this is boring", "what are we even doing here?", "OMG, 'I'm not doing anything stupid." We had spent hours designing a workshop for them and ignored their protestations, diving into our theatre games and creative exercises to engage them. Despite themselves, they enjoyed it, learnt stuff and we all had fun! Out walked a group of young women enthused, connected, and more emotionally aware.

We were offered more work to engage young people who weren't engaging with school. We started to get a good reputation for being able to reach young people who seemed unreachable. Success was addictive. "Wow," we thought. If we can support these teenagers to make real changes in their lives, we can change the world. "We've found the answer!" We were pretty evangelical in those days.

"Let's make our own company and work with all the young people no-one else wants to work with" we said. I was becoming disillusioned with the acting game anyway. My agent did not like me turning down auditions and I was getting picky! I wanted to be a part of a strong, powerful theatre, not trek to a casting to stand around all day with 40 other women, waiting to see if

I would be chosen to help sell a washing machine! I wanted to be an actor because I loved making theatre and music. Whilst I loved the theatre shows I did, touring was always exhausting and waiting for the next job did not suit me. I wanted to be out there doing things! I also wanted to have a family and children and many aspects of the lifestyle suited me less and less. I could see that what I really loved was the creative process i.e. devising and rehearsals! The process of creating something that once only existed as ideas or words on a page and turning that into a live piece.

As a child I had only ever wanted to be a doctor; a paediatrician to be exact. But I had always loved to sing and perform. Then as a teenager I saw the TV show Fame, a real 80s classic. My idols on the show wanted to be famous, and I wanted to be them! "I want what they have got – so I must want to become famous." I said to myself, aged 14. I wanted to do music, theatre, singing, and dancing. But of course, these people whose lives I craved weren't actually famous. They wanted something, and that made them vulnerable because they had to work hard at it and grow as people. I loved watching Bruno, Doris, Coco and Leroy work and learn together, working through their issues and creating music, theatre, dance. I loved to watch them shining their light; they were changing the world by working through their 'stuff' and being themselves.

"...Fame costs, and right here is where you start paying... in sweat!"

Many years later I realised I could have replaced the word 'Fame' in that iconic quote with, 'Living a Creative, Authentic Life' although it was not nearly as catchy, it was true for me! I realised I never had the slightest interest in the reality of being famous. I was a very private introvert who was extremely shy in fact and very sensitive! However, I get hugely passionate about creative potential; about humans healing their misconceptions about themselves and finding out how to live more deeply fulfilling and creative lives. I had found what I really wanted to do – I wanted to create with people and to support human beings to reach their potential; to become more of their true selves.

This Is What I Want To Do!

A small group of us decided to form our own theatre company in September 1996. We wanted to create our own theatre and facilitate others to tell their own stories and explore how they could live better lives. We were sure we could do it! We would support them to work through their challenges in a safe environment, using their own creativity and our boundless enthusiasm. But what should we call our company? This was settled when we did our first grant application form.

We had to be quick. A colleague rang and told us Boots The Chemist was offering £800 for a project with young people increasing 'citizenship' – yup, we can do that – but the deadline was the next day. We worked all day to complete the form and quoted £800 to devise and run some workshops with young women, using what we had learned from the Women of Influence project (£800 went a long way in 1996!). The application was all done, but we needed a name. Anyone who has tried to name a band, an album or a book, will know it's a really tough job. Then the name literally landed. We can't remember now who said: "Indigo Brave". I remember thinking: "Well that is a stupid name, but never mind, we can always change it after the project."

We got the job! We were officially booked. But, for reasons unknown, it was suddenly cancelled. Something miraculous happened; the brilliant colleague who had told us about the opportunity (thank you Michele Taylor), went back to Boots and got a cancellation fee. Unheard of in our business, literally before or since! Generally, you had to be already at the venue with no audience turning up to actually get paid a cancellation fee.

So, we got £400 for coming up with Indigo Brave. We thought who cares if it's silly, this is the name for us! We had our own company and were developing our own unique and creative ways of working, which we were practising and testing on ourselves all the time. Our mantra was: "We reach the young people no-one else can reach. Our name creates money. We have our own personal 42; the answer to life, the universe and everything. Bring it on."

INDIGO BRAVE'S FIRST PROJECT

As we approached the dilapidated building which had once been a school, fear gripped my stomach; I was terrified. We were actors, so if someone offered a job we tended to say yes! We had been asked: "Would you like to work with a group of vulnerable teenagers using drama and music? We need to build their self-esteem". The answer was "Yes, of course!"

The contract was to hold weekly group for sixteen-year-olds who had been found guilty of a crime – in most cases this was for drugs-related crimes or TWOCing (Taking Without Consent, otherwise known as joyriding or just plain stealing cars). We were asked to create a project that gave them something to do, engaged them and built their self-esteem. They weren't in any sort of education and were just awaiting sentencing. Imagine their level of motivation and energy for life in general!

Most teenagers have a pretty good line in 'what's the point?', but these guys had this in spades. They had already been found guilty and were just waiting to see how long they would be spending in prison. They were in no man's land, and we didn't have the faintest idea how to reach them.

We entered a cold, sterile, classic classroom with that cold, cream-tiled floor only found in comprehensive schools of the 60s and 70s, and those horrible plastic bucket chairs designed to wreck your back. Our hearts sank. We unpacked our gorgeous African Djembe drums and tried not to look as terrified as we felt. Our subjects and their 'carer' shuffled through the door looking a mixture of horrified, bored to death and disgusted.

The ten young men were completely cut off emotionally. They looked hopeless, or angry, or both. Secretly we felt utterly hopeless just looking at them; we had no idea what we were supposed to do. We had started Indigo Brave because we had had some measurable successes with hard-to-reach teenagers, but this was another level. "OK. We'll be fine, surely?" But this immediately seemed to be on a completely different planet. The voice in my head said, "We are sunk; we have nothing."

We tried to stay positive, smiley (but not too smiley.) "Let's all get in a circle." I said cheerily. They looked down at the floor with their arms folded and bodies twisted away from us; disengaged, disinterested, and pretty disgusted that they had been dragged here from their probation centre. No, they were not interested in a drama project, no, they didn't want to be there, no, they weren't interested in music, or telling stories and no, they really didn't like our stupid drums.

You did not need to be a body language expert to know that these young men had zero motivation to be here and certainly did not want to engage with any of the theatre, drama or circle games we had planned. "OK, well how about a cup of tea?" OK, fine, they would have a cup of tea – right then. We ran down to the vending machine and got tea for all of them. The best interaction we got was "thanks, but where are the biscuits?"

Miraculously, the next week we were still up for the challenge! As the cup of tea had been the only positive experience of the session, the only thing we could come up with was to try to prove we were genuine by appealing to their stomachs! We brought in our homemade flapjack and a kettle and some decent sized china mugs (no more vending machine tea in plastic cups), so they could have as much tea as they liked! We also decided to tackle the sterile classroom environment and carried comfy chairs from the staff room to replace their terrible plastic ones, and put them in our (disdainful, to them) circle and played our beautiful Djembe drums till they arrived.

They laughed at us pretty mercilessly for playing our drums as they walked in – but at least that was a reaction of some sort! They accepted the flapjack and tea. But, no, they still didn't want to do any drama games, and no, they did not want to play the drums. "We're not kids you bloody hippies!", they scorned. But they seemed to begin to believe, at least a little, that we (nutters though we obviously were), seemed to have some weird but genuine care for them. And we did, we adored all of them! All we could see were crushed, damaged young men who had been let down by 'society', abused and traumatised by 'the system' and who now felt like they had been left to rot on the rubbish heap, waiting for the inevitable.

"Create a project that builds their self-esteem" the project brief had said. We had jumped at the challenge, confident that Indigo Brave could reach anyone... but our confidence was seriously beginning to wane.

A few weeks went by and a lot of tea and huge amounts of home-made flapjack, biscuits and brownies were consumed. They still thought we were idiots, but they started to trust us just a little. They began to talk a bit in our circle. Share a tiny bit. Hold the talking stick without laughing their heads off at us. When they did, it was humbling in the extreme.

Their self-esteem was non-existent for sure, they knew they had done bad things, but the more we listened, the more the idea surfaced that 'building' their self-esteem was impossible – they were about to go to prison for crimes they knew they were guilty of. They had got caught, they had hurt people, they felt guilty, they were guilty. They felt utterly and completely wrong and furiously angry for being so wrong, and they "didn't care". Oh, how often they told us they didn't care, but they did. They really did care, but they couldn't care, because there was no point caring, no point in any of it. They were bad.

We wondered how we could go forward here.
"Don't worry, what you have done isn't so bad!" we could say. But that wasn't true; they were going to get a custodial sentence.
"Well, Ok, it was bad, but it wasn't your fault; you're a victim of the system." Not very empowering at this moment in their lives.

We settled on: "So what are we going to do with the time we have together, lads? We are here and we want to listen to you. We think you are worth listening to. We make theatre and tell stories and we think your stories are worth telling." We let them know with every cell in our bodies and every word we spoke, that we thought/felt/saw/believed their stories and lives had worth. Slowly we earned a bit more of their trust; and with more flapjack and plenty of sugar for their tea stories started coming out.

We still had no idea how we were going to complete the project brief and build their self-esteem. It did not seem even vaguely possible. When we tried to talk about any good stuff they had done, they clammed up – they couldn't remember doing any good. There were also the stories of how a few of their friends hadn't got involved, hadn't been so stupid, walked away, and not done the 'really bad' stuff.

They told how they had belittled them – called them 'chicken shits' and a lot worse. The lads who had 'bottled it' were not held in 'high esteem'. There were also stories of 'harder', 'badder' lads – the ones who had 'done worse shit', 'didn't care', 'got away with it' and 'not got caught'. The 'worse' things you did, the higher you were praised. The self-esteem picture was very confusing. We just kept listening and mirroring a place of non-judgement, of compassion, of acceptance.

Then came the session we were dreading: one of them was missing. Troy had been sent to prison. They sat still in the circle, gutted and seething angry, although they insisted, they weren't. Much shrugging of shoulders happened that week. We silently sent them love and held a space for them. If someone had been checking up on us, we would, no doubt, have been in quite a lot of trouble – we were not doing anything! But we could feel their pain, we could sense their hopelessness.

Somehow, we were determined to let them know there was hope, that their lives had worth. Troy's departure was painful. I remember processing my own feelings of hopelessness, my own regret at mistakes I had made, my huge failures, times when I wished I had behaved differently, times when I wished I could have seen some other choices. I had made loads of awful mistakes. I wondered: how was I still going? How did I have any self-esteem? What else was there when I hated myself so intensely? (And I hated myself very intensely at times). Perhaps there was something else at work that I hadn't taken into account, another part of the equation, something separate, perhaps underneath the self-esteem? A different sort of relationship with myself; a place where the bad things I had done didn't make me a bad person.

One night as I was preparing for the group, I drew a triangle. I thought if their actions were bad and inside this triangle was where their self-esteem was based, then could there be a deeper level untouched by actions, a 'being' level? Perhaps this was their worth? Not their self-esteem at all, but the deeper, supporting level of self-worth that was under it, the self-worth they didn't currently believe existed; innate, inalienable, underneath it all. The beginnings of the Indigo Brave Self Model™ was born.

The model was simple, and the Indigo Brave team loved it. We were buoyant at the next session. "Ok guys I know things look bad right now, but..." – I drew the model for them – "but your actions live here. They are separate from your worth!"

The lads looked confused; this was very alien to them. "No", they said, "we have done bad stuff and we are bad". They started to prove this to us; teachers had said it, parents, carers, youth workers. They were bad because they were always in trouble. It was simple cause and effect: they did bad things, they didn't listen, they messed up, they forgot stuff, they lied. Regardless, we firmly believed they had worth, so we decided to start building that instead.

We spent every moment from then on separating their self-esteem from their self-worth. We set out to completely ignore their self-esteem, in fact, and just focus all our attention on their self-worth. We started to agree with them. "Yup, we agree, that was a bad decision, a behaviour that caused pain; yup, you did a really bad thing there." But then we always followed up: "Now, that is strange isn't it! What would a great person like you be doing, taking a choice like that?"

We worked on our body language; you were allowed to respectfully touch teenagers back then. We offered hugs and patted shoulders when it was invited. We never took our presence out of the room for a second. We worked so hard at every unconscious cue and body language message so that we were communicating the following on every perceivable level:

- We think you have enormous worth.
- We think your self-worth can be healed.
- We see your worth as separate from your actions

Slowly, it started to have a tangible effect. We still weren't doing any drama games, and no-one had played a single beat on any of our drums, but their bodies were a little less closed; they seemed more 'inhabited'. They were definitely more present in the group. We told them we were happy to modify our grand ideas. We had opening and closing circles where we used simple structures to encourage their Emotional Literacy and we wanted to keep going with this. We asked them what would make a difference and they said they would talk while holding one of the marker pens instead of the 'ridiculous' talking stick.

We re-framed their sneering criticism of our actions as constructive feedback, and we modelled not confusing 'what we had done' with 'our worth as people'. Sometimes this was excruciatingly difficult; cool teenagers seem hardwired to be able to push our buttons and see where we had our own 'worth' tied up with validation of our actions, but we observed that in ourselves and each other and processed a lot!

As the weeks went on, they joined in more. There were some real and authentic feelings being voiced and owned. There was a vague sense that there was something else in the room, some goodness, some self-worth perhaps, and it was theirs. They were beginning to perhaps consider that they may have some good in them. We told them with every word and look that we knew they were good human beings who had experienced some very tough things (extreme trauma, actually). They had made some poor choices, but perhaps it wasn't ALL of who they really were.

Perhaps their low self-esteem was OK. It was based on an accurate assessment; it was probably appropriate. As we focused on building the worth below the esteem, it was like a deeper level became active, something that has nothing to do with deeds or actions. They all agreed that what was going on was nothing spiritual – this was made clear to us several times.

"This isn't a God thing, is it? You are not telling me that God loves me whatever I have done, are you?!"

There was no time or energy for any kind of God in that room. They had been abandoned many, many times over and God was just another one on the list of the bastards who had let them down. This was fine, we had no spiritual agenda. We were not talking about anything esoteric or spiritual at all. We knew their worth was intrinsic, we could see it starting to slowly appear. It wasn't a magic wand. They repeated the scripts we had heard many times such as:

"It was my fault anyway."
"They had to let me down."
"I was too bad."
"I was given every chance to change. I couldn't do it. I didn't want to."

Over the weeks, something was changing. They shrugged their shoulders less. They were turning up in a different way. This was when we knew for sure that self-esteem and self-worth are two completely different things. Their self-esteem was still on the floor, but they began to feel enough worth to risk telling us their real stories. It was often one-to-one, just casually whilst we were drawing, chatting...

"I hated school." "I'm not clever." "I can't do schoolwork." "The teachers hated me." "Mum told me I was useless from the start, I was a write off, I was always trouble to her."

There wasn't a single boy in there who had grown up with a dad. The group grew smaller as one by one they were sentenced and went to prison. They were crushed all over again, but their armour was a little thinner and they began to open a little more. They started to talk about how upset their mums were, the guilt that was too painful for them to even touch on, the hurt, the pain and slowly, slowly they started to voice the regret. They started to believe that, at least to us, they did have a scrap of worth. As long as – and they were VERY clear about this – they wouldn't be doing any of that pathetic drama or acting shit. "Cool," we said. "Keep on telling us your stories and we'll figure out together what you want to get out of this."

In one very powerful session, just after Jordan had been sent down (he was very popular in the group), an idea emerged from the circle:

"If I'd known two years ago where this stuff was leading, I

wouldn't have done it. I'd have backed out; I'd have got out somehow. I could have said no."
"Yea. If I could, I would go back in time and tell myself two years ago: Don't do it, don't try and be cool. It's not worth it."

We asked: "What if these stories could reach the kids who are exactly where you were two years ago?"

"Yes," they said, "We would tell them what it's really like, where it gets you. Don't do it, it's not worth it".

We worked on this idea with the six young men who were left. One liked to draw cartoons and created picture scenes. We started to create storyboards of all the times that they felt they had taken the wrong decision; right back to where the first, seemingly innocent choices had been made. Then we would take their ideas and stories and improvise some scenes, acting them out for them to watch. They were utterly merciless! Laughing out loud at our terrible 'street' accents and never holding back their disdain when we got it wrong.

But the self-worth work had developed a powerful atmosphere of vulnerability and trust. I remember a breakthrough from one lad about why he had agreed to a drug run: "I wanted the phone so bad; I didn't ask what was in the parcel. He said it was just a bit of weed and I believed him. With that phone I had some respect. With that phone everyone would shut the fuck up in that school, with that phone I was someone."

These stories eventually became the play Escape Routes. They named it; one of them said, as he sketched out a graphic scene of bullying and violence on a storyboard, "I thought I was always going to end up here, down this road, banged up. But it's not true. There were times I did have some escape routes."

The project ended without any whistles or bells. The four-month contract to build the cohort's self-esteem with a weekly drama session, ended. We had started with ten participants; we had a closure session with the three lads who hadn't been sentenced yet. We felt very emotional, and they tolerated us outwardly with even a couple of grins at the 'daft hippies'. But inside something had changed. They had a glimpse of their worth.

We promised them the stories they had told us would all end up in the play and it would get seen by young people who still had some escape routes. And we got to tell them that they had always had worth, and that they always would have. We got to say that self-worth was a birth right and we got to say sorry that they hadn't been given it.

Actually, we got to say sorry to those lads often. Sorry that the cards they had been dealt were so shitty. Sorry, there wasn't anyone there for them who could hold strong enough boundaries. Sorry their carers and the adults around them weren't able to support them better. Sorry that they were too stressed/alcoholic/busy with the babies/sad at their own losses/young/busy trying to pay the rent, and very sorry that they had little, or no, sense of their own self-worth so could not pass that on.

They also got to know they had helped create a play that we were determined to get out to the kids 'two years back'. They had done a really good thing. This didn't make them good obviously, because they were already good! They were good lads who had made poor choices and done some bad things. We got to see powerful little shifts week by week and even some small sense that there was, perhaps, going to be life beyond this sentence, and possibly a life where they might be able to do some good, because they had some good inside them. They had glimpsed their worth.

ESCAPE ROUTES:
THE TOUR

We workshopped and rehearsed our precious seed of a play, Escape Routes. We applied for funding and got a grant to tour practically all the secondary schools in Nottinghamshire for nearly a year. We performed it to selected groups of 30 young people per project, identified as being at risk of crime and drugs. We created a theatre and workshop experience we were proud of. As far as we knew it was a new concept – a two-visit 'self-awareness' experience through drama.

Visit one was a theatre show; a play that a group of three of us performed inside the school – usually in their drama studio, and sometimes in their canteen if that was all they had! It was an engaging and exciting play with lights, soundtrack, costumes etc. It also had a section in the middle where the audience got to choose the choices and actions of the protagonist and therefore how the story developed.

This was then followed by a second visit with the same group to run an interactive workshop with them. We taught The SELF Model™ practically and told them how it had come about. We supported them to reflect on the themes in the play, their own behaviour and choices. How might they change things in their life now they experienced a bit of their self-worth?

Shakespeare it wasn't, but it did have a real effect on the behaviour of the young people and gave the teachers (usually the drama or English teachers that had booked it and attended both sessions) some training in the difference between self-worth and self-esteem. All the audience saw beforehand was a leaflet advertising the play; a simple drawing of a motorway to crime with slip roads leading off to the side.

It was the story of Alex Simms, a character who could be any gender. We liked to think of them as an archetype rather than stereotype character, but they were certainly larger than life. They were a super-cool, super-tough and totally badass dude who took no shit. They disobeyed their carers, ignored their elders, broke rules, and even told the teachers to 'Fuck-off!', which always got a gasp and nervous laughter from the audience! The kids identified with Alex immediately and the story could start to work its magic.

Alex is offered a quick drug run by the super-cool big brother figure. They are offered a state-of-the-art phone. They do it - easy! They start to get some status at school. Hanging out more with the bad lads, they get involved with other stuff just for fun, low level criminal behaviour; shoplifting, joy riding, setting fire to a shed.

Then, we would stop the play and hand the drama over to the audience. In small groups, the teenagers would devise and create the next part of the story. We handed out different scenarios to each group and the choices were theirs. They always had a chance to say no to the next crime, to stop and to change their minds. In over 400 plays, created around whether Alex did the drug run/ stole the car/nicked the purse/set fire to the shed... every single group decided they would do it!

The whole audience watched each group's play, their self-esteem through the roof; shouting with bravado about how they were going to 'set a shed on fire'. Then we laid out Chance Cards and each group had to pick one – the card that basically turned their actions from low risk to high risk:

Card 1: There were ecstasy tablets hidden in the packet you carried and now you've been caught dealing class A drugs.

Card 2: You've now been told you owe the money for the phone; to pay it back you've got to do another drug run every weekend.

Card 3: There was a homeless man asleep in the shed you set fire to, and he's been injured. You're up for attempted manslaughter.

The next part of the play showed how the increased risk played out and the danger built. It showed Alex getting panicked, bunking off school, smoking and drinking and taking other drugs to cope with the stress, getting involved in more crimes to try and get more money more quickly as they hoped they wouldn't get caught... But they did.

Escape Routes always finished the same way. Alex, in court, receiving their sentence: The lights dimmed; the spotlight focussed on Alex:

The judge's voice was cold and final.

"Alex Simms; you have been found guilty. You are sentenced to 10 years in prison."

The colour would drain from Alex's face. Spotlight out, and "Cut".

In shock, the kids never applauded. It felt so raw for them because they liked Alex, they identified with Alex, they had played Alex with excitement and it had made them feel invincible, powerful, part of something. They had chosen to do the crimes and hadn't considered the risks. They were learning the consequences.

We tried to do justice to our original storytellers and recreate the effect we had witnessed when their mates went down. The shock, emptiness, betrayal.

A week later we returned to the school to work with the same group again. We played theatre games to create psychological safety and trust and then asked them to reflect on the play. Did they want to help Alex stay out of prison? Yes. They did. What did Alex need to make a different choice?

They created small group dramas of Alex trying to get out of doing the crimes in the first place. This wasn't easy to do at all! We set up the scene. An actor from Indigo Brave's company played the main 'big brother/sister' character and volunteers from the audience played the rest of the gang. We pressured and hassled Alex and when they tried to turn down the offer of doing the crime, we took the mickey, belittled, peer-pressured, shamed and blamed. We took the language from what they had shared and made it as real as we could.

The audience were given pretend remote-control buttons. They could shout FREEZE and stop the action at any time and swap themselves in for Alex to try a different angle, a different way of communicating with the gang. They could also opt for explaining their idea and have someone else act it out. They could only swap in or adapt Alex's behaviour; it is important to remember that you can't change anyone else, only yourself!

We, as an audience, watched Alex try to be strong enough to take the Escape Route, to get out. It was very rare that a group ever took the route of telling an adult. Snitching was bad news and always backfired in their opinion. But as they worked through their ideas and developed strategies, they started to see that if Alex had believed they were worthy of saying no, perhaps they wouldn't have got into trouble in the first place. Through this process they began to get the idea that with some self-worth firmly in place, perhaps they could have reached out, perhaps they could have asked a friend; "Should I do this drug thing?"

If they felt worthless it was so much harder to say "no" under pressure.

The play and workshop showed them the reality of the lads from our first group. We always told them where the stories had come from and credited those brave young men. We always finished with what became the Indigo Brave Esteem/Worth Circle. Talking about each person, supporting them to own what they could do and sharing one thing they liked about themselves, which was about who they were, their worth, not about their achievements or skills. We held the boundaries with power. No-one was allowed to diminish or belittle another's articulation of their own worth. Your self-worth is decided by you. It is not what others' think of you, it's what you think of you. And you can decide that. Your worth is yours. Don't ever give it away.

CREATING OUR OWN 'THEATRE OF THE OPPRESSED'

The feedback on Escape Routes was excellent. Not only was it a powerful way to raise the issues with young people of crime and risk behaviours, it also started to give the young people some tools to feel a bit better about themselves, their inner self. They didn't have to be 'doing well' in a school system to feel good about themselves, but we were able to give them a tiny peek, a brief but very real experience of feeling their own worth.

We were offered more contracts and started to get a reputation of working with kids no-one else could reach, tough kids with behavioural management issues. We didn't have a magic wand, but we could deliver some measurable changes in behaviour in a pretty short workshop. We used anything we thought would work; every acting, creative, expressive, therapeutic method we had in our repertoire.

We developed the technique we had used in Escape Routes, combining ideas from drama therapy and Playback theatre with elements of Augustus Boal's Theatre of the Oppressed, where the victim gets to re-play the drama that they're facing in order to change the outcome. We would have bullies playing victims and vice versa. We would talk to them about their lives, their situations, their feelings, their challenges, their loves, and their hates. They would trust us incredibly quickly and we were able to reflect so much good stuff back to them in such a short space of time. We saw huge changes in two- or three-hour sessions.

Our methodology was forming, it was always based around the fact that they had self-esteem and self-worth mixed up, and it was making their lives very difficult.

Boal says his theatre method was to "help the audience identify their internal oppressions in order to overcome them". We were seeing how the mix-up between worth and esteem was causing internal oppression, and the blame for that would then become externalised. We focused on ways we could support young people to understand the self-worth and self-esteem differentiation and the magic happened before our eyes.

One project, which contributed a lot to our understanding of this and our methodology, was when we were asked to work on a self-esteem project with a group of schoolchildren who were seriously at risk of exclusion. It was a three-month project, the desired outcomes being to increase self-esteem, which would lead to better behaviour. We asked for our usual private, comfortable space and took good tea and chocolate biscuits. We were expecting kids who were looking down, sad, locked within. Instead, in walked some of the most confident kids you could meet. We started an introduction exercise:

"What are you good at?" we asked.
"I'm pretty good at everything really."
"You can't fault me. Mum says I'm brilliant. Everybody knows I'm brilliant."

"And what do you want to do with your life?" we asked.

"I'm going to be a premiere division footballer."
"Get on The Voice and be a singer".
"Going to be a rapper."
"Play for Man United."
"Be a doctor."

"Be a lawyer."

"I'm going to be famous and have loads of money."
"How?" We'd ask…
"Don't know!"
"I'm going to be famous."
"For what?"
"Don't know, just famous!"

We called it the 'Ali G complex'. These kids had anything but low self-esteem and yet they were clearly lacking worth in a big way.

How could we tackle this we wondered?

We used our methodology of supporting them to express their world in ways that made sense to them. We started to see the pattern of a lack of self-worth being compensated for with an inflated confidence and hugely protected sense of their self-esteem. When we could support them to know their worth was theirs, that they were good whatever they did, or didn't do, then the 'false self' of the 'self-esteem front' started to fall away.

There were powerful moments in the workshops again and again when the group would see someone coming up against their own 'oppression'; their own feeling that they had no worth. We started to understand a lot more about the link between lack of self-worth and the emotional experience of shame. We observed that the feeling of shame was a feeling of worth-less-ness, or an internalised sense of being 'bad' and that this was like a black hole and once they were in it, there was no way out.

There was some truth in this. Their feelings were certainly 'unchangeable' at the self-esteem level. We witnessed the young people do almost anything to avoid that experience; run, lie, hide, blame… But when someone did feel the edge of it, or sometimes fall right in, the magic would happen so fast!

We learned to never try and fix it for them, but to relentlessly be there whilst they felt around for their own scrap of worth.

They would be supported, loved, beamed at with appreciation and deeply authentic respect for their bravery and courage. We would point out that 'many people' in the group felt the same. That we used to feel the same. We asked them to enquire into the feeling, was it really true that they were bad? We could hold them whilst they searched inside for their scrap of goodness, and they could always find something. Even if they couldn't find it all on their own, we could point to it, for them to see, feel, experience, and the group would see it too.

They would relax a tiny bit and the shame in the room would dissipate. The fellow members of the group would feel it too and start to believe and trust that, in here, their feelings and the reality of their emotions was going to be validated. We were always careful to have strong opening and closing structures and make sure they understood this was an internal experience, not one they could expect from the outside necessarily. We did not know how experienced their parents/carers/teachers were with this dynamite stuff! You can't expect anyone else to know this; you can only change you!

We witnessed that when they could see that, in here, there was real appreciation for touching the edges of their lack of worth, and it was always 'fixable' by their own experience, then they could let go of their inflated self-esteem. They started to talk about their real exam results, their real fears of failure, real incidents where they had done the wrong thing.

We brought pictures of celebrities in and talked about the addiction rates and suicide rates. We asked what makes human beings happy? We developed exercises to strengthen the separation membrane between worth and esteem. We got them to identify where they felt they could be themselves and where they needed their bravado to feel safe. We looked at the difference between being brave – built on strong self-worth – and bravado, teetering on false or unearned self-esteem.

Out in school, their behaviour changed. Over three months the teachers reported that every single member of the group improved their behaviour in the classroom and by the end of the term they were all off the risk-of-exclusion list. We got offered more work and started to train more facilitators and build our team.

We added into The SELF Model™ the idea of black holes in our self-worth, spiralling down into guilt, self-hate and eventually shame.

WORKING WITH
THE 'BAD ONES'

We didn't have too much fear going into new sessions. We always expected that they would push our buttons! Teenagers are absolutely expert at finding the places where your self-worth is linked to your actions, or even more dangerous, someone else's. What a gift! We were very clear that what we were doing was not therapy. It was learning, exploring, creative expression, but we did have clinical supervision to support us.

When we started with a new group or project we would usually ask: "Why do you think you're here?"

"We're the bad ones."
"They can't control us."
"This is a punishment."
"The teachers just want us out of the way because Ofsted are in."

"Interesting! That is not what we have been told. As far as we know you've been chosen to work with us – who are very experienced – because your school feels you have potential."

Again and again they eventually, in different ways, explained to us that their worth was tied up to their behaviour/results/achievements and they couldn't seem to succeed at that, so...? Ergo – they were bad.

Nobody had ever said to them: "You don't have to pass an exam. You don't even have to behave well. You are worthy of my time and attention". No judgement here, no-one had made it clear to their parents/carers/teachers either.

We spent the time demonstrating to them: your worth is yours. It is not dependent on what you do. How about we 'be' with you and show you that you are worthy. With sensible boundaries in place around care of self and others, you can go where you need to go.

We had pretty much free reign in these workshops, which allowed us to develop our ideas and offering. We were able to identify that most 'problem' teens had a lifetime of building their self-esteem, but nobody had ever built their self-worth. We had kids creating pieces of drama to show their teachers how they felt, making music, drumming, expressing their struggles and their world. After one course finished, a teacher met with us to say, "You are achieving measurable changes in behaviour. We need to know what it is you're doing. Have you ever trained teachers?"

OUR METHODOLOGY GREW

We had absolutely no idea how to train a teacher! How would we explain what we were doing? However, we had been asked to do just that, so we quickly became deeply interested in how we were going to develop the teacher's understanding of how we got those results.

We were asked to run an INSET day (in service training). We were very nervous. This was proper training, with an overhead projector and everything. Hand out sheets, evaluation forms, learning outcomes, whoa!

We knew what we wanted to do; we wanted to demonstrate that the concept of self-worth and self-esteem directly affected the pupils' ability to grow healthily and learn effectively. Even more importantly we wanted to show that their own understanding of the model within themselves was crucial.

We had been seeing more and more pupils being 'artificially' praised – told they were doing well, when in fact they weren't. Teachers often seemed scared of telling the truth about the results and behaviour, and we could trace it back to the mistake of having self-worth and self-esteem as synonymous. We were witnessing the creation of a kind of false reality, an ideal world where the pain of failure was avoided or denied.

We collected statements we had heard first hand from teachers:

"Everyone wins at our school."

"Everyone can get an A grade if they want."
"Everyone can go to University."
"We all win something on sports day".

We had also heard:
"8b is just a bad group, you can't do anything with them."
"He/she is unreachable."

"Are these things actually true?" we asked the teachers.

It was in the first teacher training sessions that I decided to draw the model out on an overhead projector (yup, we're going back a long time here!). I drew it the same way as I had for the young lads in our first workshop but now seeing it projected onto the screen made it more real. I included what we had been learning; self-confidence at the top of the triangle – the result of healthy (fluctuating) self-esteem being built on strong (unassailable) self-worth. The model was now open to highly trained, highly experienced professionals for scrutiny. I felt very exposed, but I knew that my worth was not attached to how the model was received, so I could be brave and plough on.

The model developed a lot through those sessions, and I am grateful for the teachers wanting to question it and picking it apart to see if it really gave them a paradigm shift they could practically use. I improved the idea of the membrane between worth and esteem and started to understand how it could be punctured if we let it, or if we had self-worth 'holes', which meant the membrane wasn't really there at all. I included the dangerous little black holes in our self-worth; spiral vortices that could pull painful experiences into themselves, (if the membrane was weak in certain places). If these self-critical voices could get into our worth and find some purchase, a place where we feared these beliefs about ourselves were true, they could spiral down building energy as they went making the shame experience excruciating.

Although we deepen our understanding of how this model works with every client's unique perspective, it hasn't fundamentally changed much since those days! The three-tier triangle with confidence at the top, self-esteem in the middle then self-worth underneath, has never let us down. We explained that if you have no self-worth then there is nothing to prop you up when your esteem crumbles (perhaps appropriately) because things had gone wrong.

Some teachers reflected that they might be getting their self-worth needs met by the pupils; for example, how well the children behaved, so if the children behaved badly it affected their own self-worth. There were a few tears, some aha moments and recommendations to work in other schools and even education conferences. Our teacher training sessions taught us how to work with adults and all the training, conference, and board level workshops we do today started there.

STRONG AT THE BROKEN PLACES

Concurrently to this, and on the back of our 'measurable changes in vulnerable people' results, we were asked to run some projects with people with long-term mental health histories in day centres. The people we met had been depressed for decades. We ran the workshops we'd developed and quickly realised they needed this model, but the beliefs and behaviours were more deeply ingrained than in the young people and teachers. How were we going to reach them in a way that was meaningful?

We applied for some money from the mental health charity, Mind, and won a grant to create an Escape Routes inspired project for adults with long-term mental health issues in Nottinghamshire and Leicestershire. We used the same model, running workshops and, with permission, collecting real life stories which the theatre company then created into a play called Strong at the Broken Places, a story about a journey from mental and emotional illness to real emotional and mental health.

We met so many amazing people with incredible stories and watching them learn that their self-worth was their unassailable right was unbelievably moving. I remember vividly one woman we met in a mental health day centre group in Leicester. She was severely anorexic, and her best friend had recently died of anorexia. She was absolutely going the same way. Every centimetre of her arms and most of her legs were covered with deep self-harm scars. She loved our play and in the workshop that followed it had a breakthrough and life changing moment.

Decades later she is now fully recovered and – through her own incredible efforts and huge amounts of determination – qualified as a nurse and now specialises in mental health.

We toured Strong at The Broken Places to just about any organisation or day centre that would have us and the word spread. The play showed that your self-worth holes, i.e. your broken places, can become a source of understanding, compassion, forgiveness and self-love. A wounded place, but also a place where you can become stronger than you were before by integrating it, healing the pain, and learning its wisdom.

The play was about two women. One coped with her lack of self-worth by acting out and drug use, eventually becoming mentally ill. The other coped with her lack of self-worth by 'acting in', becoming super good and caring for everyone else, eventually becoming a mental health care worker.

I played the 'bad one'. Imagine me, if you will, in Doc Martens and a biker jacket saying: "If I can't be good, fine, I'll be bad. I can be good at that!" The play looked at the parallel lives of the two characters as one goes through the full diagnosis and enters the mental health system, and the 'good' character works in the mental health system but is still acting from a place of need to help people in order to feel like she has some worth.

Again, Shakespeare it definitely wasn't, but we had some wonderful set design, directors, musicians and writers working on the project. It was an engaging play, demonstrating that we all have mental health issues and showing the lack of self-worth that so often underpins them. It was a very powerful vehicle.

In the play the characters eventually meet and become friends and start to understand how much they have in common. The audience members with mental health issues tended to love the play, while some of the carers found it extremely challenging. It definitely suggested that mental health is not something that happens to others, and implied we all have mental health journeys, no-matter what our position within a perceived hierarchy.

Strong at the Broken Places was a pretty 'out there' theatre show but, the most important part of it was the participation workshop that followed, where the audience got to experience that whatever your mental illness and diagnosis, you still had unequivocal self-worth and that everyone, no matter who they were, has some self-worth issues.

The play/workshop tour continued, and we were thrilled when Indigo Brave became the first theatre company to be asked to perform at Rampton, a high-security psychiatric hospital in Nottinghamshire. We went for the preparatory meeting with the Governor, who explained Rampton's status as a high security hospital/prison. The show and workshop would be for an audience of women, and we felt honoured to have this amazing opportunity to reach people who may not have had access to theatre for years, decades... perhaps ever.

The play was due to go on at midday and we arrived in our transit van with the set, costumes, make-up etc at 9am to do the 'get in'. We had been well briefed that we could take nothing that was sharp and had carefully modified our set accordingly. Security took the van apart and went through everything with a fine-tooth comb. I remember they confiscated my tiny Body Shop eyeshadow Twilight Teaser because it had a mirror in it the size of a thumbnail. Nothing sharp meant nothing sharp.

We entered a canteen area where we set up and waited... and waited. We were told they wouldn't be able to say when it would start – we would have to wait till the women were allowed in. Eventually 30 women came, sat down and we began our play. It was only about an hour long and we got an amazing reception straight away. The workshop usually started straight after the play. We were excited to start and began to arrange the chairs into a sharing circle. The women were gathering round and almost shouting their stories at us: "You've just told me my story." "I took drugs after I lost my baby." "I never met my baby."

The women seemed desperate to share their stories. The level of trauma was overwhelming. Then suddenly, just as we were beginning, an alarm went off and the guards started moving the women out. "There's been an incident, everybody goes back to their cells." We protested, seeing how much the women needed the workshop: "We haven't finished - we have to do the workshop!" I pleaded.

The guards stared at us with a look that said: Do you know you're in a prison?! "But the workshop is the most important bit!" we said. The response: "They've had enough, that's plenty." (I don't think the guards enjoyed the play).

The number of women trying to talk to us was heart-breaking. We got to speak to a few. "That was my story" they said over and over. Thank you, thank you they said. They loved it. We were alone in the canteen, very moved and devastated not to finish the process. We had to wait in this colourless box room until the guards came to collect us.

It was the hardest show I've ever done in my life because it didn't finish. Those women didn't get to hear that: "Whatever they've done, they were still human beings. They were people. They had worth."

We began the lengthy process of getting back out through security. I collected my Twilight Teaser eyeshadow in its labelled plastic bag at the gate. We'd been there the whole day for a one-hour performance. We just hoped it had done something.

We took the pain of it all to clinical supervision. We came to the resolution that it was better to have done the small bit we did than to not do anything and we can't know the far-reaching effects that that might have had. We had to surrender to the idea that it was good enough, something is better than nothing.

We got to examine yet another place where we were potentially feeling good about ourselves because we were 'doing good things'. Was this yet another self-worth hole? Once we discovered it, we could heal it. We learnt a lot about the place the action comes from being as, or even more, important than the action itself. We went back to our model and saw the level of self-acceptance the model helps to imbed.

We could see that 'confidence' to act in the world comes from a place of self-worth; being worthy already, then the esteem to be gained or lost from the action going well or otherwise is kept out of our worth. We had done what we could and that was enough. It hadn't been as much as we had hoped, but that was OK. It wasn't a failure of worthiness. It was just not as much as we had hoped or would have liked to 'do'.

The whole experience brought us to a greater level of humility. Perhaps we can't change the world as quickly as we thought. Perhaps we can just do our little bit. It taught us a lot about the things we can control and the things we can't. My Nain (my Welsh Grandmother) bought me a bookmark with The Serenity Prayer on it when I was nine years old.

"Please grant me the courage to change the things I can change, the serenity to accept the things I cannot change and the wisdom to know the difference."

Yup, she knew me.

WHEN THE HOUSE BURNT DOWN: AKA WHEN I GOT TO REALLY PRACTISE THE MODEL!

We were very happy in our top floor flat (more like a bed-sit actually). Many aspects of Indigo Brave were born there including many creative projects and the odd play! But we wanted to start a family, and for that we needed room. In 2001 my husband and I bought our first home together. There was a big allotment at the end of the garden, which, when we arrived, was a derelict tip! We cleared it, put fences in and added raised beds. It took a lot of hard work, but it was our little paradise. We grew fruit and vegetables; carrots, cabbage, all the usual stuff, plus some less usual – grapes, red, black and white currants. We had a polytunnel where we grew tomatoes and the most incredible cucumbers!

A lot of happy memories were made in this house and garden. We had two children; we lost a baby too, in a late miscarriage. We named her Gabrielle and planted a pear tree in the garden for her. We built a chicken house and had gorgeous chickens pecking around the fruit trees (we soon learnt not to let them into the veg plot.) We built a wooden cabin in the allotment and our home and the land around it became our wonderful retreat.

Indigo Brave were working in education and mental health as well as training future leaders in SMEs and global companies. Our business was affected by the 2008 crash, but we had enough flexibility and projects running to pivot and enough people wanted our work for us to keep going. Things were good.

In April 2009, a very strange thing happened; we looked out of the bedroom window at the back of the house and saw our shed was on fire. We rushed outside, but it was too big to put out. We called the fire brigade and apologised a lot for calling them out just for a shed, but they said we had done the right thing and though we had lost a lot of stuff, it was only stuff and we thought little more of it. Every now and again we heard a rumour of another fire on the estate.

Then, four months later, whilst we were away on a camping holiday, we received a phone call from our neighbour to tell us that our beautiful cabin, which we had built in our garden, had been set on fire. Although he acted quickly and called the fire brigade, it was gutted, and we lost the roof. It was our meditation space and spare room. We lost beautiful and irreplaceable possessions like tapestries and other beautiful objects from our travels around Laos, Cambodia, India, Thailand, Australia and New Zealand. It's difficult to explain how shocking and deeply sad this was for us. Much sadder than losing a garden shed!

In April the following year, our wheelie bin was set on fire – not the first wheelie bin fire in our neighbourhood. Weeks later there was another fire in the alleyway between our house and the house next door. The flames licked the roof of our lean-to at the side of the house; we were beginning to feel like our house was under attack. The police attended the scene after every fire but were drawing blanks. Groups of neighbours and people gathered on the street after the fires – there was a lot of talk about needing to 'take things into our own hands'. I remember one guy shouting: "If anybody sets a fire on my property, he won't know what has hit him."

As all the fires had been started between 10pm and 2am, my husband started to patrol the area with other men from the estate. The patrols began with ten or so men but eventually dwindled to just my husband, Mathew, and the neighbour's son. One week later, on May 13th, 2010, Mathew was exhausted from patrolling for the previous six nights. He decided he was too tired to patrol that night, after all we reasoned, he couldn't just patrol forever, and there had been no fires for a while. We fell into bed and were fast asleep by 9pm.

At 11:45pm there was hammering on the door: "FIRE, FIRE, GET OUT!" We leapt out of bed as the smoke alarm started going off. I went to pull the children out of their beds. I was super conscious, moving quickly but totally calm and super alert. My daughter was three and didn't take kindly to being woken up, she started to cry, "Darling, we have to go now", I said. Something in my voice must have registered with her, she stopped crying instantly as I picked her up. I woke her brother in the top bunk and he also responded to me, just quietly climbing down the ladder without complaint; very unusual!

We started to walk down the stairs, the window at the bottom of the stairs blew in. It's hard to describe the noise of a fire that has really taken hold, it's very, very loud. Flames blasted through and my son dropped my hand and ran back up the stairs where smoke was now pouring in from the top window. I grabbed him and said: "No, love, we have to go now."

Mathew had gone out the back and started to try and tackle the fire but quickly realised it was pointless, the fire was too out of control. He came back through the house, carefully closing all the doors behind him – we knew a lot about fires by this stage and were aware this would slow the blaze. He followed us out the front door. The fire brigade took exactly four minutes 30 seconds to arrive.

Later that night at a neighbour's house Mathew and I were sitting on the sofa.

Mathew said: "We've lost the house. We've lost everything."

I looked at my family around the room. "One, two." I gestured toward our sleeping children. "Three and four." I counted him and me. "What else is there?" I asked him. "All that is of worth to me that was in that house is this room."

He smiled and we sat there in the dark, listening to the children breathe and feeling very, very deeply grateful and content.

"We do have to record an album though." I said.

"Dear God," he stared at me. "The house has just burned down, if you could not make a 'to do' list right now that would be great." We started to laugh hysterically.

"No, seriously," I said. "If we had died in that fire, I would only really have one regret, and that is not having the courage to have recorded our music. So, I am going to stop wishing I sounded like Annie Lennox, or Robert Plant for that matter, and we are going to record the music we have written."

"OK, deal," said Mathew. "But first let's sleep."

I couldn't sleep. I was in shock. The following day the insurance company found us a hotel down the road with a family room for the kids, but I wasn't really sleeping at all. I went to the GP and told him my story.

"How many happy pills would you like?" the doctor asked.

I picked up the prescription and put the generous supply of pills in the cupboard, but I didn't take them. I thought to myself: "If Indigo Brave's models work, now is the time I try them out. Now is where I walk the talk."

The Day After the Fire

As I returned to our still-smouldering family home a policeman walked towards me. He looked like the classic stereotype of a 1970s detective in a brown, ill-fitting nylon suit. Mind you, no judgement, I looked a sight! I had had very little sleep, and someone had just set my house on fire. I was wearing borrowed clothes and I can guarantee I had not brushed my hair. "Morning Luv," he said, eyeing me with a strange indifference. " Is this your house?"

"Good morning, yes it was", I answered. "How do we stop this? How do we catch this guy?"

"Oh, well Luv, arson is always very difficult to solve," he began.

I saw red, I took a deep breath and said:

"No. Stop right there. I have heard for over a year now that "There's nothing you can do" and "Arson is a hard crime to solve". Are you telling me that if an MP's house had got burned down you would be saying you can't really do anything?! No, you wouldn't be! We are going to find the person who set my house on fire. We are going to remove the long-standing threat of arson from this whole estate. We are going to solve this crime. And also, I don't want you to call me luv."

That police officer spoke to me differently from that moment onwards. He turned out to be an amazing ally and, in the end, worked so hard to solve the case and bring it to trial. I still have his number in my mobile phone.

Nottinghamshire Police had just come out of the league tables as the worst police force in Britain. Their esteem was on the floor. So, I set about working with them, using the Indigo Brave principles. Every time I came into contact with one of the team working on the case, I made sure they knew I had faith in them. I took every opportunity to let them know I believed 100% that they were going to solve this crime. When things went wrong (and oh, how things went wrong), I let them know I believed in their positive intent.

"I know you are a good person doing a difficult job and I know you can solve this crime. How can I help?"

I always worked with their mistakes at a self-esteem level. I held the belief that they were great people with a very difficult job. In the 12 months before the case came to trial there were some enormously challenging moments. They lost the ONLY eyewitness statement, but I just kept using the model. I never got angry with them; I insisted on believing that they were all great, worthy equals and we could do this. We dealt with the esteem-level issues that needed to be addressed. The investigation went on and on. They were very nervous telling me they had lost the eyewitness statement. I remember saying: "OK, (deep breath out...) how do we get that eyewitness statement back?" What I was saying was "I know your worth has nothing to do with this."

I took responsibility for all my feelings and took them away with me. I shouted, screamed, danced, drummed, I even piled up cardboard boxes and smashed them up with a baseball bat. The stress and anger and frustration and pain were there, but I expressed them out of the situations I was in. That way it didn't get into my communication with the police. I couldn't afford it to be there. There was too much at stake. We had to be an unshakeable team and although they didn't believe they could solve this, I did.

Ten days after the house fire, the police arrested the suspect. It was the son of our next-door neighbour. He was eventually charged with 10 counts of arson. There had been 17 fires in the last two and a half years. From that point on there were no further fires on the estate.

The suspected arsonist's parents did not think he had set fire to our house, or indeed that he had set any of the fires. Neither did his sister or wife, both of whom lived in the house with them. We didn't know if it was him either. It was a strange feeling. We had lived next door to them for nearly 10 years. We would go back to the house to oversee the builders and his family would watch us, twitching the curtains. We just wanted whoever had done it caught, and safely behind bars, before someone was hurt.

Even though we were living in a rented house by this stage, we had to return often to show the insurers round, or police, or to oversee the builders once the work was started to rebuild it. Other people on the estate told us that the family blamed us for his arrest and believed that we had got their son into trouble.

The house did get rebuilt and we moved back in in January 2011, eight months after the fire. After living in a friend's house, two hotels and a rented house, it was lovely to be back in our home. The suspected arsonist was out on bail and told not to come onto our road; instead, he would park on the road leading up to our street and stare into our window.

"There's nothing we can do unless he comes onto the street," the police said.

No-one knew if he was guilty or not at this stage. We practised a belief that his behaviour reflected his self-worth holes. Sticking with our model saved us a lot of stress, overthinking and heartache. I could maintain my compassion for the suspect and his family by using self-worth and self-esteem exercises. I told myself that setting fires was just what someone had done, not who they were.

It was easier to hold a solid belief in the suspected arsonist, than it was the insurance company. This was my biggest test. After the fire, the insurance company immediately began an investigation on us because in Britain, arson is the most common way of defrauding insurance companies. Despite a suspect having been arrested, they accused us of burning the house down because that way they wouldn't have to pay out. I had to work very hard indeed to hold positive intent and self-worth with the insurance company!

But I treated them in the same way as I did the suspect; their actions weren't who they were. I could see that everybody is trying to get their needs met. If we communicate with the part of them that's trying to get their needs met, then we can make sure we are separating their worth and esteem – even if they can't do that for themselves yet.

Be it an insurer who's treating you like you burnt your own house down or a police officer who rings you the evening before the trial to say: "I want to manage your expectations, Laila. I don't think we're going to get a conviction here. We'll be lucky if we get 3 out of 10!"

The trial was meant to last four days, but it was still going on eight days later. We gave our evidence. We didn't stay for the verdict, but the jury did find the suspect guilty of nine counts of arson, including one count of arson which endangered life. Although he pleaded not guilty, there was no appeal launched. Thirteen months after the fire he went to prison; we hoped he would receive the help he needed. We put our house on the market the next day. We had tested our model to the limit, and it had worked. We realised that the model was a hugely effective tool to communicate with people and get the absolute best out of them whilst being truly authentic.

The power of holding the truth of somebody's unassailable worth and emanating that through thought, body language and tone of voice was very powerful. People's abilities to do the right thing grew. Their doing was built on their being – and when they got something wrong there was an energy underneath to support them to fix the mistake. They were good people, and what if everyone was still a good person, no matter how badly they messed up? We realised that this was a powerful way to make forgiveness and compassion live within ourselves and a practical way in which to give it to others.

"I've already seen the bottom, so there's nothing to fear." Pink

After the fire it was time for a new chapter. We had always dreamed of living in an eco-house, to live closer to nature, raise animals and grow food, perhaps even build a centre for people to come and experience Indigo Brave's work in an environment where all the elements were reflecting their worth, others' worth, the planet's worth.

So, no more watching Grand Designs we were going to do it! We searched high and low and eventually found some land we could live on and in September 2011 we moved! We lived in a wooden cabin and mobile caravan with no electricity and two small children, and we could even find real gratitude for the arsonist's actions (not that I would even wish the experience on anyone) because it had made us reach for more; to not get comfortable! We had reached the point where we had nothing else to lose, so we set about building the life we'd always dreamed about.

I understood that this was just stuff that's happening to us. Our worth is not diminished because we've lost everything. Nothing that has happened to me happened because of who I am. I understood that our worth as human beings is who we are and the genuine connections that we have. Our knowledge around self-worth and self-esteem kept us going during a year of extreme turmoil, stress and grief.

I don't want to give the impression that it was easy or smooth all the time! I got angry, furious in fact. I tried numbing the pain with red wine and chocolate for a couple of months, that just made me feel worse and put weight on too! It wasn't that I didn't have emotions about what had happened, what was happening – I had loads. But I did not turn those emotions into 'blame' of the other person; of their worth, of their being-ness. Instead, I brought those emotions home as mine. My power. I used them to build my resilience, to get fit.

I joined a gym for the first time in my life and joined a Body Combat class. I supported my back to get stronger and heal, I even got a personal trainer. I railed and shouted, I criticised and judged, I insulted and ridiculed... but only in the gym – whilst kicking and punching the pads in front of me being held by my 6ft-plus trainer, who grinned at me: "Come on Laila, is that all you've got?" Oh, I experienced all my emotions, but I used them for me. I didn't 'waste' them on the other people in 'my story'.

The model kept on working, and I kept understanding it better and better. Not only did it support us, but we also journeyed through those months with compassion and understanding for ourselves, each other, and the people around us in all the craziness of human beings. We forgave the insurance company, the police, and the arsonist, not from a place of superiority but from a place of knowing their worth was the same as ours. Who were we to judge their actions? We had no way of knowing why they did what they did. It wasn't our business.

There was no way I was going to resent any of it. We came out of the experience richer with deeper understandings of how our Self Model™ could work in the most extreme of life's challenges and it had made the grade. The anti-depressant pills never left the cupboard.

PART TWO

THE SELF MODEL™

What It Is, How It Works And How You Can Use In Your Own Life

This section of the book will take you through The SELF Model™ in more detail and show you how you can use it to build your own self-worth and manage your self-esteem. Firstly, just in case you have jumped straight to here and not read part one of the book, let's look at how we can *know* that self-worth and self-esteem are not synonymous.

Are you struggling with the idea that self-worth and self-esteem are different? I'm not surprised if you are, we have always been told they are synonymous. But worth is about our 'being'. Esteem is about our 'doing' level of existence.

Our dear friends have two daughters. Lillie was born with cerebral palsy. Lillie can't 'do' anything on her own; she can't stand, she can't walk, she can't sit up.

Her little sister Rafi does not have cerebral palsy. She is full of boundless energy! She is into running, dancing, climbing, drawing and singing.

Who has more 'worth' – Lillie or Rafi? Which child is 'worth' more to her parents?

It's so clear! No one has ever answered anything but "Both daughters have the same worth." Lille is breathing; therefore, she has worth. The fact she can't do the things Rafi can is not relevant. Rafi and Lillie are both amazing; loving them, and being loved by them, is an honour in my life and a wonderful experience.

Rafi knows exactly what she wants and what she likes and who she is; as does Lillie.

Lillie has clear and passionate preferences; as does Rafi.

Lillie has a wicked sense of humour. She is uniquely Lillie, and she is a wondrous human being – just like Rafi.

Rafi's gifts are easy for the world to see – she is a very 'out there' kind of a girl!

Lillie's gifts may not be quite so obvious to the casual observer, but if you can take a moment, drop into your being-ness and really 'be with' Lillie, her gifts are awesome, and you may be able to receive them. Lillie has nothing to prove, nothing to achieve. If you are lucky enough to get a smile from Lillie, or even better, she laughs at one of your jokes, your whole world lights up.

We can clearly understand that the 'worth' of these two lovely girls has nothing to do with their ability to 'do'. And hopefully that has sparked some curiosity about your own 'beingness' versus your own 'doingness'.

Let's explore more deeply how The SELF Model™ helps us understand the difference between self-worth and self-esteem. The following diagrams show how self-worth is the foundation that supports self-esteem and together they build self-confidence. The diagrams also show two other important concepts: self-worth holes and the membrane that prevents self-esteem issues from permeating and damaging self-worth.

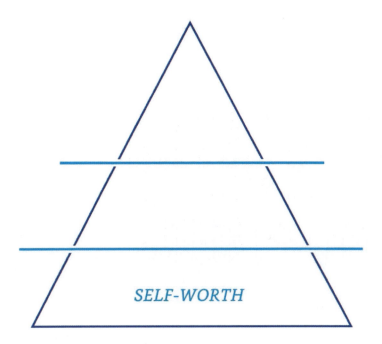

SELF-WORTH

This belongs at the foundation level of existence - our beingness.
It is different to self-esteem and should not fluctuate with
our actions.

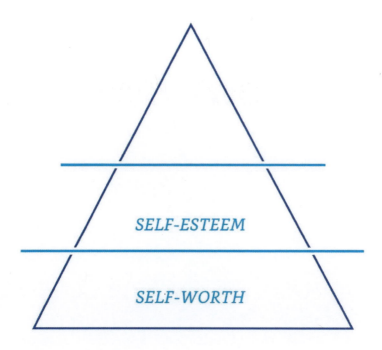

SELF-ESTEEM

Because self-esteem is about what you DO, it is based on how you feel about your own behaviours, actions, abilities and habits. Therefore, it will always fluctuate with how well you are (or are not) doing.

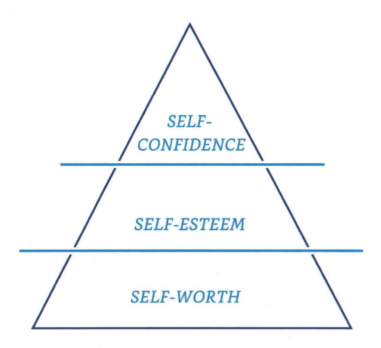

SELF-CONFIDENCE

Self-confidence is at the top of our triangle and is built on healthy self-worth AND healthy self-esteem. Many people build their confidence on their self-esteem alone, which is flawed.

The word confidence comes from 'confide', the latin words which mean 'with trust'. It literally means to have trust in yourself.

So, our self-confidence is how much we trust ourselves to 'deliver' who we are, out in the world and our abilities to contribute to the world.

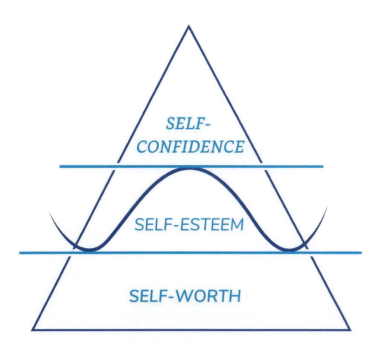

FLUCTUATING SELF-CONFIDENCE

Healthy self-esteem should naturally go up and down. We need to be able to evaluate our esteem depending on how well we are doing at any given time. Sometimes we do great, sometimes not so great!

If our confidence is based solely on our self-esteem then our confidence will fluctuate with it. This may not give us an accurate enough picture of how confident it would be appropriate to be. We may have too much or too little to operate authentically and effectively at any given time.

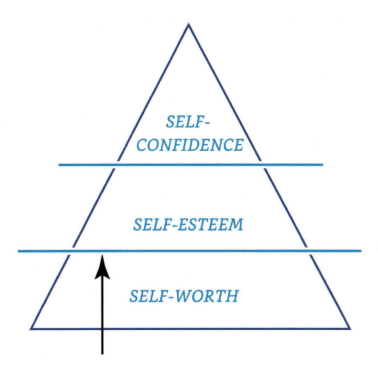

THE MEMBRANE

It is of crucial importance to have a membrane that separates
your self-esteem and your self-worth. This 'membrane' is the key
to making sure you do not allow any self-esteem drops
(caused by real or perceived mistakes, failures, wrong doings),
to affect - in any way - your self-worth. It is simply nothing
to do with your self-worth. Your innate worth is as a breathing,
living human being. End of.

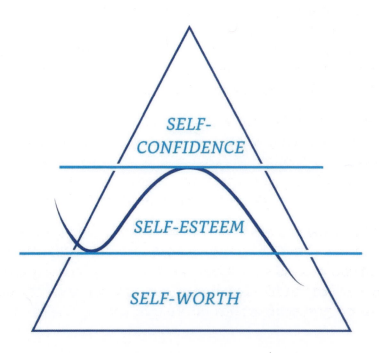

AREAS OF WEAKNESS IN THE MEMBRANE

If we do not have a strong separating membrane between our self-esteem and self-worth, then when our self-esteem takes a dip (which is inevitable and healthy), that healthy 'ouch' feeling of not doing our best can get into our self-worth. At a self-esteem level that feeling is a desire to do better, some learning of how we let ourselves down, perhaps some healthy guilt. However, if it gets into our self-worth it turns to shame. Strengthening the membrane can be a tough job, but it is essential. I go into detail on how to strengthen the membrane in the following section where I discuss the model in more depth.

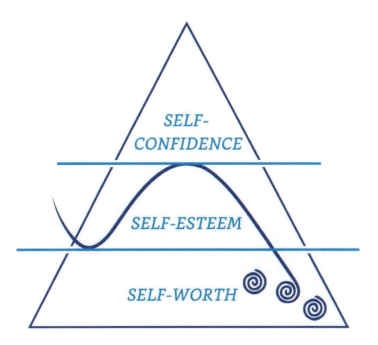

SELF-WORTH HOLES

Everyone has self-worth holes. They are 'woundings' of our self-worth, often covered up for years (decades), by holding our self-esteem up. I see these as 'black holes', spiralling energy, drawing us downwards to worse and worse thoughts, stories, feelings and imaginings. If we do not stop them, they can lead us down a spiral of worth-less-ness. We may have devised coping and numbing strategies, but this does not take the holes away. At the end of this spiral is always deep unworthiness and shame. In the following pages (after the model) I'll talk more about the different types of shame and guilt and how they create these 'black holes'.

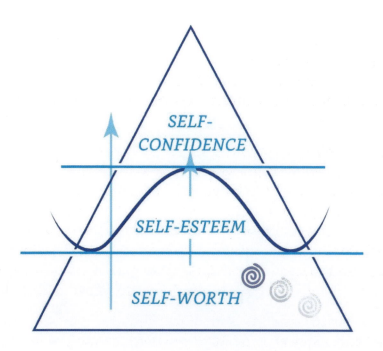

MENDING YOUR SELF-WORTH HOLES

Of course these 'black holes' need acknowledging, mending, healing and filling up from the inside. Numbing or trying to fix them by doing something 'good' will never work. Read on and I will show you how to heal the self-worth holes.

Self-Worth

Your worth as a human is not the same as your self-esteem. Your self-worth should not fluctuate; it should be unassailable. You have worth simply because you exist; you are a unique, amazing collection of biological cells that make you a living, breathing being. No matter what your worldview is, no matter what your beliefs are, you are part of this universe at this time, and you have worth simply because you are. There is nothing that you could ever do, good or bad, that can take away from that.

You could consider your self-worth to be like a solid rock as a foundation for your life. Your self-worth is simply your 'you-ness'. As you feel into this you can start to 'know' this foundation and, whilst it does not change, your sense of it can certainly be strengthened and reinforced. Your self-worth is your own innate capabilities, qualities and values, such as your sense of humour, kindness, empathy, tenacity, caring nature, love, creativity.

Self-Esteem

Your self-esteem, by comparison, is not rock-solid. It is more like water. It ebbs and flows as we move through the challenges of life. Sometimes it is a low tide and sometimes it is a high tide. This is normal and healthy. If you accept that it is ok to have fluctuations and go with your flow, it is much less problematic. The ebb and flow of self-esteem is usually driven by your actions (by what you have done or have not done), by your thoughts about the actions you have or have not taken and by the consequences of those actions. We simply can't get it right all the time, so if we can meet the reality that our self-esteem drops with an action that 'was not of our best', or a mistake we have made, then we have a far better chance of changing our actions next time.

Self-Confidence

In the model, self-confidence sits at the top of the triangle. Confidence is about self-trust. Do you trust yourself? Do you trust your choices, your actions, your feelings, your intuition, your resilience?

There is a lot written on building our self-confidence and it is a vital element in becoming really effective in the world as your level of self-confidence directly relates to how well you can present yourself to others. However, I'm sure by now you are starting to appreciate that, if our self-confidence is built solely on our abilities and actions, then our self-confidence will be only at the self-esteem level. This means that if/when our self-esteem drops, our confidence drops with it.

However, when our self-confidence is also based on our immovable self-worth, then our confidence is supported by that 'foundation level' of the triangle and if/when our self-esteem drops in a healthy way, our confidence does not collapse. This view of self-confidence means we do not have to always artificially hold our confidence up if we don't feel it, because we know our confidence is supported by a strong sense of self-worth and the acknowledgement that self-esteem will fluctuate.

This is great news as our sense of self-confidence does not depend on having a good self-esteem day; you can have a self-esteem nosedive, but still have confidence in yourself to get up and go again. You may have not performed your best and lost confidence in an ability or skill, got something wrong in a relationship and lost confidence in your ability to communicate or lost a job and lost confidence in your value to society, however, if your self-worth is known to you and your sense of it is well developed, then you can reach down into it and build your confidence from there.

It is very hard to truly feel confident about anything if your self-worth is wobbling or non-existent. Working on that solid foundation of self-worth is a pretty critical factor in your capacity to feel confident in any situation, whilst being able to acknowledge that mistakes may have been made, skills may need learning or improving and/or changes may be needed.

If your self-esteem is high that naturally feeds your confidence, of course, but this way you can remain confident and acknowledge your vulnerability based on your solid sense of your own unassailable self-worth. And all this can be maintained, regardless of whether your self-esteem is flowing or ebbing.

The Membrane

You can see by looking at the model that in between the self-worth and self-esteem 'layers' there is a line, this line represents what I call 'the membrane'. The membrane protects your self-worth. It stops your 'doing' from interfering with your 'being'. However, 'good' or 'bad' your actions are, who you are remains protected and unaffected. Therefore, if you make a terrible mistake, you can get back up and have another go.

The membrane is there to stop the effects of our actions becoming who we are. If we perceive our actions as bad, wrong, stupid, failure... etc, and then we let those perceptions penetrate into our worth, the risk is that we start to believe (and let our subconscious mind start to believe) that we are bad, wrong, stupid, a failure.... etc. This creates toxic shame in the physical/emotional/mental system and is truly poison to a healthy 'self'.

Just in the last couple of hours my self-esteem has been up and down like a rollercoaster. This doesn't happen all the time, but when it does it is not a problem, it is in fact very healthy. In the old days one of my many downward journeys of self-esteem would have led to me taking a chunk out of my self-worth because there was nothing separating the two. But that does not happen now. I have a strong membrane that stops any feelings about what I have or haven't done from getting into who I am. My membrane does not allow it. It also prevents me from filling any holes I may have in my self-worth by 'doing' more good things (or apparently good things).

What is also important to notice is that when we allow positive feelings of self-esteem (i.e. our ability to *do* something good) to make up for feelings of low self-worth then we are encouraging our worth and esteem to enmesh and become the same. In other words, we are weakening the membrane. This gives the false idea that we can feel more worthy and be a better person according to what we do – and we should avoid this. If I give to charity to make me feel that I am a good person, but I am resentful as I do it, then it will not make me a good person. I am still the same person with the same physical, emotional, and mental system that I had before.

Doing good does not make you good. You can *be* good and *do* good, with good self-worth AND good self-esteem, but doing good per se does not make you a good person. We know this, in fact we have a phrase for it – The Do Gooders – and it's not a compliment!

The integration of this truth is the first step in the development or 'mending' of the membrane between the two types of self-ness. When being and doing are aligned, you experience *flow* state – the doing is almost easy, inspired even, because your actions are coming from your being. And that's why it is a very clever semi-permeable membrane – from self-worth to esteem it can flow, BUT if we are trying to fill a 'hole' in our self-worth with things we are DOING, we get the following: imposter syndrome, narcissism, self-doubt, Picture Reel Living, perfectionism … and it will never work. You simply can't fill a self-worth hole with esteem!

As I was writing this book, I was discussing the model with a friend who is a professional biologist. He was interested in why I was calling the separation between worth and esteem a membrane. It had stuck in my head from biology class at school – it's a non-permeable membrane in this direction, I explained (you can't mix esteem and worth), but it is permeable in this direction (worth can increase our confidence and appetite to build our esteem and 'do' more and 'better' things).

He explained that the membrane I was describing actually does exist and is called a selectively permeable membrane. This type of membrane recognises the proteins it wants, and the proteins it doesn't want within a cell. It was amazing to me that the science of the biological membrane works perfectly when applied to The SELF Model™, even though it is a model and not a biological organism!

Self-Worth Holes

Self-worth holes occur when our sense of our own self-worth is anything other than solid, impenetrable and can take anything that life throws at us. I think most of us have self-worth issues of one sort or another. If the membrane is weak between self-esteem and self-worth, then issues with our self-esteem can get into our self-worth holes and cause us real problems. Self-worth holes can really spiral downwards. The narrative accompanying that drilling down sounds like this: "Oh, my God, Laila, your ideas are not good enough." "You always say stupid things…" "You've done it again." "Why would you think you could ……. blah blah…" And it invariably ends up with "What is wrong with you?" or "Why can't you be better?"

If my membrane wasn't strong, and the critical spiral was initiated and then allowed to carry on its downward journey and puncture a hole in my self-worth, I'd reach this: "I'm worthless". This is a downward spiralling journey I don't wish for anyone. At its worst, the consequences of this downward spiral can be life threatening. I had a friend who took her own life; her note said: "I'm such a drain on everybody. I can't do this life, and everybody will be better off without me." That's the epitome of zero self-worth. Her membrane was non-existent, she believed her life mistakes were her identity. Every 'bad' thing she did or 'bad' feeling she had got right in and reinforced her negative self-worth and reinforcing those negative spirals.

If we don't protect our self-worth from the natural, healthy dips in our self-esteem, our self-worth holes spiral downwards into self-loathing. In the past, when I made a mistake, I would find myself thinking: "how awful, I've messed everything up, what a terrible person I am." After nearly 30 years of work, I can say: "Wow, that's quite a mistake. I have not done very well there. I forgive myself so that next time I can do it better." I'm able to do that because I have strengthened the idea of always keeping a membrane between my self-worth and self-esteem.

When we have a strong membrane, it can protect our self-worth at all times and the dips in self-esteem become more manageable. It's perfectly healthy to allow yourself to build your confidence up through a healthy self-worth membrane, but nothing gets down through it. It is a very clever piece of kit! How Can We Strengthen the Membrane?

To strengthen my membrane, I had to become strict with myself on what was worth and what was esteem. If I did something well, I naturally went through the normal feelings: glad, thrilled, happy, even proud. But I would also take care to consciously remind myself that it didn't make me worthy. "This does not change my worth. Nothing I do changes my worth." Sometimes even now I remind myself. "Don't let the good self-esteem feelings get into your self-worth. They are different!" I coined this silly phrase to help me remember.

"If you take the hit, you'll end up in the pit".

This reminds me not to allow the positive hit of "I've DONE something well" to affect my worth. I know that if I do then I am compromising the membrane, and that runs the risk of esteem and worth getting mixed up again! And if/when I come down from a big success, then I will end up going much further down from esteem into worth and end up in a pit of despair if that thing I've done (or something else) goes wrong.

What phrase might you use to remind you to separate your self-worth and your self-esteem? Write it on a sticky note (or several) and keep it where you can see it.

Another effective process we can do to strengthen our membrane is to dig deep into appreciating our qualities, values and innate beingness that is the foundation of self-worth. These are not our learnt skills or the things we can do/achieve or own; these are qualities such as our sense of humour, our inner beauty, our capacity for compassion, our love of nature etc. Qualities that would still be part of who we are regardless of what we do.

When I first started to make these distinctions, it was a challenge. I started at the back page of my journal. I headed the page with:

If I can't do anything, what are my qualities?

I invite you to do this too. It may take a while, but you don't have to do it all at once. Keep adding to the list as the quality comes to you.

It took me a week to find the first one: a sense of humour. I don't have to do anything to have an innate sense of humour. The second was love. I am love. I feel it within me; it is part of me. Being loving is just something I am.

After I'd made a start, I could work with ideas that were harder for me like 'I'm beautiful.' That was a really tough one for most teenage girls growing up in the 80s, (and still is, though the understandings and pressures are different). But I worked hard on my list, and one year on I could name fifty qualities.

I only allowed myself to include it on my list when I really believed it and could feel it was absolutely true. When I had named these qualities and considered them, they became more tangible and real for me, and I could feel them filling out the worth section of my triangle so that my esteem could elegantly go through its normal fluctuations.

Perhaps you would list your appreciation of others, or your full sensory enjoyment of your favourite food, your love of animals, or your loyalty, compassion and kindness towards your friends.

Self-worth is not measurable, and that's its value to me. That's GOLD. While we are in a society that turns everything into a commodity, it's radical to say that you're worthy just the way you are. Let's be radical together!

What Does Covering Up A Self-Worth Hole Look Like?

When somebody's trying to prove their worth to you, they are covering up a self-worth hole with self-esteem. I have met countless people who are spending their lives like this. They are often highly successful, driven, able... but they have a deep concern that they are not worthy of this success, and it could all disappear overnight. I believe mixing up your worth and esteem is one of the powerful causes of imposter syndrome.

In our competitive and frantic corporate world, it is very easy to believe that a feeling of a compromised sense of self-worth – a self-worth hole – can be compensated for by creating more and more self-esteem. But this will never work. It is a seductive trap and can become addictive. You cannot fill a hole in worth with esteem. It is like trying to fill a swimming pool with sand and expecting to be able to swim in it! They are simply different substances, and they are not interchangeable.

I have worked with many, many highly successful executives, right up to CEO level, who believe their worth is the value they can create for their company. However, if you are trying to create financial worth to fill a self-worth hole, you can get addicted to wanting more and more. The hole is a bottomless pit and 'more' will never be enough.

I remember working with a super-achiever Commercial Director in a big company who said: "I have low self-worth, but I need it. It drives me on, powers me forward, without it I would stop pushing myself...." I worked with him on the understanding that, whilst there may be some truth in the 'sensation' of being driven, using low self-worth in this way is like filling your car with very dirty fuel. It may have been driving him forward, but it was having a very nasty effect on his 'vehicle' long term! Over time he learnt to use 'cleaner' fuels to drive him forward e.g. life purpose, legacy, vision and mission. He learnt to separate these motivators from his self-worth and found that contrary to his fear that his drive and motivation would disappear, his motivation increased. He became less fearful and anxious, and he allowed himself to also spend more time with his family. He reported his relationship with his wife was transformed and his general satisfaction and happiness was much, much better.

Can Your Self-Worth Holes Be Healed Or Even Close-Up Completely?

Yes! Absolutely they can. As soon as you stop trying to fill up self-worth holes with self-esteem, they become much easier to heal, creating a more solid foundation of worth. It can be painful to see where our sense of worth is missing, and that means healing it is not necessarily easy, but we have seen thousands of people over 25 years make a change. They have either been able to take the concept on board quickly for an instant paradigm shift, or work on it consistently, weekly, painstakingly digging away at their self-limiting beliefs. Often, they have needed both. I certainly did. The lightbulb moment of the insight, the shift... and then the preparedness to keep on observing where I had mixed up self-worth and self-esteem, and a conscious dis-entangling and healing of the different energies.

When we find a hole, a belief that there is something wrong with our very being, the first thing we must be brave enough to do is to recognise it; to see it and own it as ours, even though we may be very invested in denying its existence. After all, it is not cool to believe terrible things about ourselves, to believe that we are not a worthy person, but until we can see it, we can't do anything about it! Once we can own the hole, we can see if that belief stands up to honest enquiry: is it actually true? And then it is imperative that we do the work to heal the hole.

What if you notice the self-worth holes of others? Have compassion and hold the belief that they too can heal. Remember that they are not their behaviour. Hold a loving space for them in your heart. It is not up to you to point out the hole (unless perhaps they have asked you to, or there is a professional relationship e.g. you are their coach), but you can hold the space for them to discover, own and heal it. This is especially true if the person is your spouse. Remind yourself that their self-worth hole is not directed personally at you. Do not let your self-esteem or self-worth be influenced by someone else's – hold them in love and attend to your own healing, e.g. what feelings/emotions/reactions does their lack of self-worth trigger in you?

Case Study

For over 10 years now, Indigo Brave Social Enterprise has run a weekly group open to (but not exclusively for), people with long-term mental health histories. It is open to anyone and in its current incarnation is called Gardening for Wellbeing. It is based on permaculture principles and biodynamics and is a safe environment for people to learn about sustainability through working on the land, whilst being accepted as they are. There are some simple ground rules for safety but apart from that, people can do as they choose; be loud or quiet, active or lazy, emotional or not. They can turn up with no judgement or expectation that they should be anything other than themselves.

People grow and change here. The methods are simple, and the successes powerful. People have found their confidence and gone on to let go of anxiety and move through depression, to find employment and/or healthy relationships. Some have found the courage to follow their dreams and relocate, or just simply feel better, more of the time. There are too many success stories to share, but here is one of our favourites:

Pete's Story

When Pete started to attend, he had had severe depression for many years. He'd sit in a chair, too tired and weak to manage much gardening. When asked how he was feeling he would reply, "I have been to the shop this week." Going to the shops was his achievement, his way of saying that he was a worthwhile person.

One week he was late arriving and was desperately apologetic and on the verge of a panic attack. His opinion was that being on time made him a good and worthy person and therefore when he was late, he must be bad. He couldn't see what we saw: that Pete was here with us having triumphed over considerable challenges and setbacks. We recognised his worth to be beyond the 'failures' and 'illness' he believed he 'was'. Pete is patient, compassionate, kind, understanding and willing to talk to anyone about anything. We saw his worth. "We just care that you're here, Pete." we said. He couldn't believe no-one was angry or upset or just a tiny bit judgemental or passive aggressive about his tardiness.

At the end of the year, we hold a 'Self Circle' where we invite feedback from members about what they appreciate about each other. Each person spoke directly to Pete, sharing how much they appreciated him on both an esteem and worth level:

"I love it when you praise my planting skills."
"I consider you as a father figure."
"You're always so kind and encouraging."
"You listened to me and made me feel that you're interested in what I had to say."
"I love your generous spirit."

Pete was nothing short of amazed. "Nobody has ever said anything like this to me," Pete replied, tears in his eyes. After a year of attending our group Pete started to believe that he has worth, just for being him. He is less depressed and anxious, and now volunteers for the group, helping others to feel their worth and grow their confidence and esteem.

SHAME AND GUILT

How These Affect Self-Worth And Self-Esteem

We all suffer feelings of shame and guilt from time to time. However, there is healthy shame and there is toxic shame, and these can impact our self-worth and esteem in different ways.

Healthy shame is the understanding that we are only human. We are not always going to get it right, it's not possible, it is not the way we learn. We have so many other pulls, agendas, energies, emotions and conditioning. Healthy shame is our 'Jiminy Cricket' character from Pinocchio. It's our conscience. The little voice saying: "I don't think we are living up to who we truly are." It's a way of us being able to notice that we may not have behaved in a way that feels good to us. It is not a judgemental feeling, it is an "Oh shoot. That wasn't my best".

It's also worth stepping back for a moment to look at perfectionism in this context. In its toxic form, perfectionism is not an irresistible drive to achieve the best possible result but more a pathological desire to avoid making any kind of mistake. Often perfectionists do not allow themselves to make mistakes of any kind. People with this kind of personality NEVER get things wrong – but the stress of always trying to get it right can be huge.

This also led me to make the same differentiation with shame. Toxic shame is deadly. It is a crucifying, excruciating feeling. It is like a thick, suffocating fog, filled with toxins that get into your body and create pain. It stops you breathing fully or thinking clearly. It is like having your brain crushed from the inside out with the toxic lie that you are worthless. It is the experience of literally 'being' wrong at our level of existence. A deadly feeling that has nothing to offer us except for our learning to spot it and stop it.

Toxic shame says, "I'm wrong therefore I'm bad." This spirals to: "If I'm bad; I have no worth. If I have no worth, the tribe is going to exclude me." In human existence just a few centuries ago, that would mean dying alone on a hillside. This is why teenagers agonise over the peer pressure of wanting to belong – their limbic brain tells them that if they don't belong, they'll die. Not if they don't belong, they might be open to a new set of friends. Toxic shame = death. So of course, it is to be avoided at all costs.

Healthy shame is operating at the level of self-esteem but does not affect self-worth unless it seeps into a self-worth hole. Toxic shame on the other hand is most definitely the product of, or the creation of, self-worth holes. Dealing with toxic shame and perfectionism means looking deeply into those self-worth holes to see what is really going on and addressing the issues that are causing the shame to arise.

I believe the same can be said for guilt. It has a healthy form and a toxic form. The difference between healthy guilt and toxic guilt is the understanding of where that guilt is coming from. Healthy guilt is "I've done something wrong, but I have the power to make amends." Toxic guilt is "I have done something wrong, and I will never be able to fix it or make up for it. I can't change the things I have done; therefore, I will never be able to do anything good again. I cannot forgive myself."

The difference between healthy shame/guilt and toxic shame/guilt has been taught to me a million times by my amazing children. This has become more and more obvious as they have entered their teens, but they were teaching me long before that.

CHILDREN AND TEENS

This is a huge topic and as this book has grown it has become clear that how we parent and facilitate children and young people to develop their own solid self-worth and healthy self-esteem deserves a book in itself. So that book is in development!

What I will say here is that parenting our own children in this way has been eye opening, revealing, demanding, challenging, and incredibly rewarding. Parenting in a way that always supports the right of the child to be themselves, even when it doesn't suit us as parents! Parenting without coercion; without the go-to tools of bribery, manipulation, emotional blackmail, punishment, shaming, and generally giving them the idea that something in them is wrong. It has meant having to take responsibility for our own emotions and not put them on to our children. It has been a phenomenal journey and as they grow into their late teens and adulthood, it continues to be so!

It led to scenarios like this one, which was etched in my memory from when our son was about 14 years old.

"Could you take the rubbish out please, Luke?" "No, I don't really want to do that Mum."

Instantly I am upset. How dare he say that! Doesn't he know all the things I do for him?! But I don't say that. I say:

"I hear you don't want to Luke, and I would like you to do it."

"And I hear you Mum, but basically, I'm listening to myself, and I am saying 'No, I really don't want to do that right now'."

I remember my feelings are mine. I breathe and remember that this isn't personal. I take a moment to admire his total lack of need to please me and glory in the fact that his self-worth is so solid that he feels almost no need to gain my approval at a self-esteem level. He knows he is loved at a self-worth level and that is immovable. I keep breathing and inwardly celebrate the parenting success we have managed. I then explain that I understand the point he is making and that the consequence of him taking that choice will mean that I will now cancel his mobile phone contract, which I pay for in return for the household jobs he agreed to do.

Luke takes the rubbish out.

It was not always as calm as this from either side! I have real and very healthy shame around the fact that lots of the time I am not nearly as calm as I appear in this example. But it is not toxic shame. I am a great mother and a good person, who sometimes loses the plot and behaves in a way which is contrary to how I want to behave. When this is with my kids it hurts. I hate it. But I still do it. I am a work in progress trying to live up to my potential!

This work comes with a health warning: if you take on the responsibility for your own self-worth then you can't get it from your children anymore and you will likely end up with very empowered young people! My children are aware that their feelings are their responsibility, but they also know my feelings are my responsibility. When your children don't need to win or earn your love via their behaviour, then you lose a huge tool in 'making' them behave in a certain way.

At four years old Esmée's passion was princesses, she spent her days wearing a white Cinderella style ball gown despite the fact we lived on a muddy farm. When Monday came around and we'd need to get Esmée ready for school, it was time for her to wear the lovely and practical smock dresses and leggings I wanted her to wear.

"I'm not wearing anything unless it twirls," she'd protest. I'd get her dressed, turn around and she had taken her clothes off. One morning became famous for us both. It took us 20 minutes to get dressed. She'd had at least three different outfits on. Finally, we'd got her into one that was acceptable for us both. I turned around to leave for school, and she was standing in her knickers. As I looked in shock, Esmée looked at me and said: "Now, Mummy, don't make yourself angry."

There was no way she was going to take responsibility for 'making' me angry. Because of this work I couldn't say: "Esmée your actions have made me angry." My four-year-old had stopped me in my tracks. Even though at that moment I was fully triggered, it was still going to be my choice how I responded to my daughter. I love my children to their bones, but I do not always manage to stay patient with them and sometimes I lose it and then I YELL! I am a Welsh Dragon at the heart of me and if I am pushed beyond what I can manage I lose it!

Being a parent is simply the hardest job in the world. It is also incredibly rewarding. The book on parenting will give this topic the time and space it deserves. For now, I will say this; I honestly believe from observation and experience, that working on a healthy separation between your own self-worth and self-esteem is simply the best way to support children, young people, or anyone, to become responsible for developing their own.

It is essential to support all young people to differentiate between self-esteem and self-worth. When we can support our young people to find out who they are, what they love and the qualities they bring, they feel and see their intrinsic worth. Where you have young people in your life, please share that they are unique, enough, and worthy just as they are. Teach them that their self-esteem can fluctuate and that's ok. Encourage them to keep a list of their qualities as a reminder of their wonderful beingness. We work with teenagers every year and it is still shocking to see how many of them already have deep self-worth holes. Let's help them to heal those holes before they have to carry them into adulthood.

THE DIFFERENCE BETWEEN WORTH AND VALUE

The terms self-worth and self-esteem are currently used interchangeably and, as we have seen, this causes some issues. As I mentioned at the beginning of this book, worth and esteem both have roots in words that mean value. Superficially, this can create something of a paradox when we use worth and value synonymously, e.g. something's value is it's worth... But is it? We must be very careful if we assign this idea of 'value' and 'worth' being the same to human beings. If we imply that we can take an assessment of the worth of other human beings, we are down a rocky road. Does one human have more worth than another? As we have already established with the story of Lillie and Raffi, the answer to that question is no.

Does one human have more 'value' than another? Well, that depends on how you are defining value and in what context. For the purposes of this book, we are going to say that self-worth and value are two different things.

Our value to society or to other people is not the same as our self-worth. The amount we can give, earn, produce for our community, contribute to our family, neighbours, or the world has a value. But that is not our worth. Also, our net worth (which you can assess on a spreadsheet) is not the same as our self-worth (which you definitely can't).

Begin to watch for where people, systems or organisations put a value on your worth. Does it lead to you placing a discrete judgement on your worth? I do not believe worth has a sliding scale. There is no more or less when it comes to the worth of a 'self'. It simply is. You can breathe, be, sense and love, you are beautiful, you are you. That is enough. Particularly watch for the insidious temptation to get our worth from the opinion of others – even lovely others who really want to help:

"I'm worthy because my partner says I am."
"My kids think I am a good mum...   I'm worthy because my kids say I am."
"I'm worth something now I have this fabulous new... outfit/sofa/car/award." (Delete as appropriate.)

These things have nothing to do with self-worth. It is a cliche to say these things won't make us happy, but it is true; they won't. Fleetingly and superficially happy perhaps, but I believe that is a misunderstanding of what happy really is. Deep self-compassion and self-love is real joy and therefore offers happiness for me. And that comes from fearlessly separating my worth from my esteem and restoring my connection to the 'inner spring' of self-love which bubbles through me to heal and 'fill' my self-worth holes. Nothing external can ever fill a self-worth hole effectively.

Self-Forgiveness And Compassion

I am in awe of people who seem naturally self-compassionate. I have had to learn it. But through the learning process, I have found that self-compassion is very easy to say and very hard to do. When the SELF Model™ is truly working in your life, then self-forgiveness and compassion simply flow. They are not an action that you have to do. They arise within me because I am able to drop into my self-worth and forgive my mistakes, transgressions, shortcomings and failures at the self-esteem level. I can't tell you where it comes from, but it is a wonderful feeling.

I like to think of self-forgiveness and self-compassion like the beautiful flower that appears in all its radiant beauty after a lot of hard work behind the scenes. I always remember this when I see the first snowdrops; one day they just seem to appear. We don't see all the work that has been done through the year. All the sunlight and water needed to feed the bulb, storing all that energy through the summer, autumn and winter, the nutrients from the soil that were absorbed getting ready for the crucial moment when the shoots push up through the hard, cold earth, and there it is, the beautiful pure white promise that spring is on its way again.

Compassion has come because I have done the work of holding myself accountable without taking chunks out of my worth. My forgiveness of my mistakes always comes with a tinge of regret, but a bigger gratitude for the learning. As a client of mine says: "I forgive myself so that I can do it better next time."

Have you heard of Kintsugi? It is the centuries old Japanese tradition of mending broken pottery by filling in cracks with gold and making them stronger and even more beautiful than before. That's what this work is about. I am a big fan of becoming stronger and more beautiful at the broken places.

When you can separate your self-worth from self-esteem, you can see the holes in your worth much more clearly. This means you can mend them and, when you have, they will be golden, beautiful and radiant.

You can't change things about yourself and imagine that would still be you. You are you and there is no other. And the beautiful paradox is as soon as you can accept and live that truth, then you are freer to truly grow and develop – to be more of you.

Working with The SELF Model™ is peeling off the layers of conditioning and nonsense put on you by a society that wants you to feel lacking in some way (so it can sell its pre-packaged solutions to you). Once you know how wonderfully worthy you are – just as you – it's much easier to let the real you out. You are enough just as you are. Radiant and wonderful, failing and vulnerable, you have worth.

So, let's turn our attention to some practical ways you can use The SELF Model™ in your own life, get to know your self-worth and learn how to manage your fluctuating self-esteem.

PRACTICAL EXERCISES TO USE THE SELF MODEL™

Maybe the stories so far have resonated with you, and you are already seeing places where you can sharpen your thinking around your worth and esteem? Or perhaps you can't yet see how you could make this a real and valuable tool to create the life you want and increase your success?

I believe you can. The first step is to start ask yourself this question: How am I defining my self-worth? This is an intensely private question, as only you can answer it and it is really no-one else's business. To do this you are going to buy yourself a journal and meet a new friend!

Building Your Own Self Practice

Differentiating between self-esteem and self-worth is just the start of the journey, and the difference can be subtle.

The following exercises are designed to help you build your own practice of checking in with your 'self' on a regular basis. Using your Self Journal to write down your thoughts and insights is a great way to track and celebrate your progress. The exercises won't work just by you reading them, they really do need you to do them. Go on, have a go!

Journaling With Nojo

Treat yourself to a new 'Self' Journal.
Whether or not you journal regularly, buy yourself a new journal or notebook just for this work; it is a precious journey into the depths of you and how you see/feel/interpret and communicate with yourself. Make it a real gift to yourself, a beautiful, practical, smart, perfectly sized, pleasing to pick up, Self Journal – whatever speaks to you. Something that you would buy as a gift to someone you appreciated, i.e. you!

Meet your new friend… Your NoJo!
Your NoJo is your non-judgemental observer; a very powerful ally in the journey you are on. The name arrived during a learning workshop with our team at Indigo Brave and it stuck! Your NoJo is a quick and memorable way for you to be in touch with your 'witness self' – the part of you that can observe your thoughts and knows, utterly unshakably, that you are not your thoughts. Let's understand this a bit better by talking about what it is not.

It is not one of the thoughts or voices in your head telling you what you should or should not be doing, or what you did or didn't do right or wrong! It is not your inner critic, nor is it your inner angel or best friend, who is always on your side. The NoJo is not your conscience or your judge (do you remember the characters on the shoulders in the old cartoons?).

The NoJo is the part of your mind that literally observes what you are doing with no judgement, good or bad, at all.

Here's some real-life contact with my NoJo that I 'feel/hear':
I notice you are eating bread again, Laila, and I notice that you said you didn't want to do that.
I notice you haven't been for your cold-water swim yet, Laila.
I notice you are feeling anxious about speaking to this group of leaders, Laila.

I notice you are feeling frustrated again, Laila.

You get the picture.

I love my NoJo. It is the most important tool in my own self journey. I experience my NoJo like a cool, calm waterfall of a voice; ever gentle and clear, offering wisdom with no agenda. It took me a long time to hear her (mine is she) in the moment, especially if that moment was a heated one! She is always observing me with kindness, clarity, accuracy, and utter acceptance.

She is the part of me that is aware of my thoughts. The part of me that can always see that I am more than my thoughts, feelings, behaviours, so that I can truly observe them and see they are mine but not all of me. Then I can be free to ask if I believe what I think is happening; in a way I can investigate and question if the thought and/or feelings I am experiencing are 'true'.

As Byron Katie points out, it is not our thoughts that are the problem, it is believing them that causes the issues.

Some meditation traditions use the witness self, and you can investigate this idea more if it has grabbed your attention. But you don't need to. Just remembering that you have a NoJo will get you started!

I have had clients draw pictures of their NoJo, and some are animals, cartoons, fantasy figures, and clouds! How does your NoJo look/sound to you? How would you represent this part of you that is totally and utterly accepting, serene and non-attached to outcome?

Draw or write a description of your NoJo in your new journal.

Determining And Defining Your Own Self-Worth

On the first page of your journal, write a sentence welcoming in your NoJo.

Let them know that you welcome their observations, that you believe they are 100% on your side with no judgements. Write that you are on a Self Journey, and you are genuinely grateful for any observations they might have as to what your thoughts, feelings, emotions, sensations are doing at any point. Explain that you are now embarking on learning how those thoughts may be mixing up your self-esteem and self-worth, and you want to receive the wisdom of the observations your NoJo might make.

Then in your journal, record what you notice. What do you hear when you listen to your NoJo's voice? What words of wisdom do they share with you?

Take a moment to reflect on these questions and answer them for yourself in your journal. There are no right answers, no-one will ever read this. It is for you and you alone.

Recognising Your Own Self-Worth Holes: Notice The Small Stuff And Extract The Wisdom

You can build your sense of your self-worth cognitively, by recognising the shift in thinking that this book offers, and that is great. But if you really want to heal and build your self-worth, you must first be able to recognise your self-worth 'holes'. Then you need to be brave enough to name them and be willing to repair them in a way that will support those holes to properly close and heal, rather than just stop hurting.

However, it can be a subtle art form to really get to grips with recognising and naming our self-worth holes. We are trained and re-trained to ignore them and cover them over so that we can't feel them, and other people can't see them. This means that when we do come across them our powerful instinct is to cover them up as quickly as possible and hide/run/fight as quickly as we can.

We've been told not to sweat the small stuff and, in terms of worrying over tiny irrelevancies in our lives, I agree. But our emotional life is not small stuff. Some would argue it's about the biggest stuff there is! I'd like to share an example of a 'small stuff' incident that led to a big discovery for a client.

Maggie's Story:

Maggie boarded the bus home from work after a long day and handed her ticket to the driver. "This is the wrong ticket. Trying to scam a bus fare?!" the driver scowled at her. Maggie had mistakenly handed over an old bus ticket and felt deeply embarrassed. Maggie 'ought' to have been able to handle this situation with a response like: "No, you misunderstand me. I had no intention of buying the wrong bus ticket and I'm very sorry for an innocent mistake." Instead, Maggie felt embarrassed and struggled to find the ticket she had bought.

She did find the ticket and the bus driver let her get on, but she then sat on the bus feeling everyone was looking at her. She tried to ignore the feelings and pushed them away, criticising herself for being so stupid as to let a little thing like that get to her.

However, she had been set the homework of noticing her emotional life and was engaged with watching for her self-worth holes. So, when she got home, instead of her usual pattern of just letting the thoughts churn over somewhere in the background of her head: "horrible bus driver - how could he have been so mean, it wasn't my fault", mixed with, "stop thinking about it Maggie, it's (you're) ridiculous", she took notice. She stopped and wrote down what was happening. This led her to realise that underneath the normal embarrassment was some old toxic shame. She traced it back to an event in her childhood when she had been accused of cheating.

Maggie had found a self-worth hole.

Set yourself the task of noticing small things that cause a feeling of embarrassment or being uncomfortable, upset, or little 'ouchies' in your emotional life. Commit to recognising them and writing about them to discover what is underneath. Could it be toxic shame? Perhaps from long ago? Then use the *Be your own coach* exercise next to clear out that toxic shame once and for all.

Be Your Own Coach

This exercise can become an invaluable tool in your toolbox for growth. I use it for all sorts of enquiry when the 'voices' in my head are loud and need listening to. It enables me to physically separate myself from the voices so I can enquire into how valid they are and what they are trying to tell me.

Fundamentally, it just involves you using physical space and chair(s) to allow the voices to 'have their say' whilst you can hold a place of unassailable self-worth to enquire into what the voices are telling you.

Below are detailed instructions for using the technique for a strong version of this exercise, looking specifically at shame. I have detailed this one because it is the toughest! When you can do this one, you know you are really filling those self-worth holes with shimmering, crystal clear, healing 'water' from within (and decorating any leftover cracks with pure gold).

You are going to become your own no shame/no blame coach.

If you start this exercise and experience overwhelm, then stop. If you start to feel too many emotions or any sensations that you don't feel you can handle, then stop. Toxic shame can be hard to clear on your own. If this exercise is too overwhelming on your own, you may need a professional coach to support you with it. If it is uncomfortable rather than overwhelming, then you may have a friend who could support you. Any trusted friend can help (especially if they have read this book). It is very important that you do not re-shame yourself, so be mindful of that.

You will need two chairs opposite each other, paper and pens (I like big felt tips).

Write a list of incidents or times when you felt shame. Choose one situation to work on and write it on the paper. Focus on just one situation at a time.

Sit on one of the chairs, holding the piece of paper. Feel the feelings of how it felt at that time and the thoughts and beliefs that the incident brings up. Stand up and leave the paper – and the feelings – on the chair. Now walk over to the other chair and become a combination of your wise self and best friend. Look at your 'shame' on the other chair.

Listen in your head to the things you said and believed about that incident. Listen carefully to what your 'inner self' believes about the situation and then speak (I like to do it out loud) to yourself, as your coach. Mirror back to 'you' what you hear/see/feel from the coach's vantage point. Why did you feel shame? Was it toxic shame? Did you believe it made you a bad person? Was it a healthy shame? Did you believe you had crossed your own value system?

From your coach-self, ask yourself: Are there some Grains of Gold hiding in the sludge of feelings? Did you make a mistake and are feeling regret? Breathe into that. Can you feel and release that regret? Can you see that you were doing the best you could at the time? Then you are just feeling healthy shame. Keep breathing... let the emotion move within the light of acceptance and love from your coach.

Your coach knows you inside and out. Your coach knows if you were doing your absolute best, or if you let yourself slip. Either way, there are things to learn, and you can learn them. Go and pick up the sheet of paper from the other chair. Sit there and feel the appreciation and love of your coach-self. Let that love in. Let yourself be seen as yourself, just exactly as you are, perfectly imperfect. You are not omnipotent, you are not superhuman. You simply are not going to be able to be your best self every minute and you are going to get it wrong sometimes.

Self-forgiveness is vital. Sit and release the emotions. Listen to your body. Listen to your coach-self – what do you need to do? Move, stretch, dance, shake, make some noise, sing, tone, cry, laugh, roll on the floor, wiggle your legs in the air like a tiny baby, (these are just a small selection of things I have done in this exercise!)

If you want to read more, I recommend *Healing the Shame That Binds, and Reclaiming and Championing Your Inner Wounded Child* by John Bradshaw.

Allow Yourself A Month Of Judgement-Free Mistakes

I once put myself in a process I named Mistake Month. I was allowing mistakes and would celebrate them for a whole month. This is reframing. Before Mistake Month, as an unhealthy perfectionist, I would agonise over making the right decision. In my first week of Mistake Month, I was going through Nottingham Victoria Centre on my way to an appointment when I saw a gorgeous coat in the window of a shop. It was tailored at the waist, and knee length. It was a wow! coat. It wasn't on sale, I hadn't planned to buy a coat, I hadn't spent weeks considering what kind of coat I really needed. My internal dialogue was going into overdrive:

"I love that coat…. BUT: What if the coat is too warm? What if the coat falls apart? What if I can't afford it? What if it really doesn't go with my other clothes!? IT ISN'T EVEN ON SALE! Surely, I can't just buy a coat!!! What if it turns out to be a terrible mistake..."

However, it was Mistake Month! I thought to myself: "If the coat turns out to be a terrible mistake I'll celebrate it - Yeah! Brilliant, a mistake! On the other hand, it could turn out to be a really great coat."

Mistake Month meant the decision was far less agonisingly difficult. I was able to talk to myself in a far kinder way: "If you go home and decide it literally is the worst garment that you have ever seen then you can bring it back and celebrate making a mistake."

Mistakes were ok! This was my cure for perfectionism. Incidentally, the coat was fabulous, and I loved it and wore it until it literally fell apart. But that is not the point. It could have been a terrible mistake – and that would have been OK too. When you spend your life having to get things right because if you don't get it right you die in your own shame, there's no room for mistakes.

I could bypass my toxic shame with Mistake Month. I had no shame attached to decisions or outcomes; everything was celebrated. After Mistake Month I began Mistake-Six-Months, which followed on to Mistake Year and now Mistake Life. That's how I recovered from perfectionism.

Pick your month and do it! It is powerful stuff. Remember to journal and use your experiences to develop your recognition of your emotional reactions and when/if you are mixing up what you do with who you are.

The Key To Discovering Your Self-Worth Holes Is To Notice What Triggers You

Notice if you're still holding a worrying/churning/cycling thought about a triggering situation hours, or even days, later. Start to allow yourself to name shame in your feelings and/or body. Healthy shame is much closer to strong embarrassment. It is not a pleasant experience, but it passes quickly. Notice the difference between that and an experience of toxic shame. Note your experiences in your journal.

Notice Disproportionate Reactions, Clean Out And Heal Those Holes!

When I wake up at three o'clock in the morning with a situation replaying in my mind, then I am not having a proportionate reaction to that situation. After all there is nothing I can do about it at 3am! It is in the past. There may indeed be things I need to do the next day, new insights etc., but what I need most at 3am is sleep so that I can be at my best the next day. Disproportionate reactions, e.g. losing my temper over small occurrences, are a really important indication that there may be a self-worth hole causing a 'black hole' effect and creating perceptions of 'dreadful' things, which, upon clear reflection, are not so terrible after all. My self-worth hole is usually underneath that reaction, looking for (and perceiving) 'evidence' out there to 'suck' in energy through any potential weakness in my membrane.

I can now see any disproportionate reactions as an opportunity! They are a sign! My NoJo can spot them and it is a gift, as I can see that there is a self-worth hole that needs healing. I can then create some time and space to investigate what is there and what needs clearing. I will invariably find some more feelings of toxic shame or guilt.

Write a list of anything that causes you toxic shame, get out your pen and get cleaning out that brain-dust! Keep a notepad by the bed in case you ever get those 3am wide-awake moments and carry a notepad with you when you are out and about. You can even write it on your phone, but I suggest you translate it to your journal; you use different parts of your brain typing and handwriting.

Psychological Storc (Sustainable, Temporary, Organic, Recyclable Container)

Most people have some brand of stackable food storage containers in their kitchen. Being a child of the 70s I well remember those famous Tupperware Parties and the excitement at the new kitchen equipment that would revolutionise women's lives (yes, kitchenware was women's business in the 70s). These days I am not a fan of single use or non-recyclable plastic. In fact, I try to ensure I can live without any plastics but, being a flawed human being, I fail regularly. So, for this exercise let's create the perfect storage container – a STORC!

- They are recyclable
- They are organic and individually designed by you
- They live in your mind

My psychological STORCs system is hexagonal and colour coded. What style are yours? If you feel so inclined, draw a stack of your STORCs in your journal.

Here's how we use them: think of a situation that brings up toxic shame for you. Notice it, name it, and put it in a psychological STORC in your mind. You could also write it in the stack in your journal.

This is not locking it away or forgetting about it; this image/idea is specifically based on food containers, and you can't leave them in your fridge forever. Open your container as soon as you have the time and space to process it. You get three days or maybe a week at most, but anything you've stuck in a STORC really needs to be opened and dealt with by then, otherwise... well you know what happens to that forgotten container at the back of the fridge.

Journal and ask yourself: what's underneath that? What are the belief systems that are causing you to be vulnerable to this toxic shame? It is likely you will have a whole list of beliefs that are not true.

Byron Katie's 'The Work' is very useful here. You will find it freely available on the web. It is so simple and basically uses four questions. For each self-limiting belief you ask yourself:
Is that true?
How can I absolutely know that it is true?
How do I react when I believe that thought?
Who would I be without that thought?

Then come up with a sentence or statement that is the opposite of your original thought or belief. How does that change your perception of that belief? What new insights do you have? Note it all down in your journal.

Seeing Yourself Through The Eyes Of Your Best Friend

This is a powerful exercise, with many incarnations. Here's a story I love from Elizabeth Gilbert:

"I walked into an office building one afternoon in a hurry and dashed into the waiting elevator. As I rushed in, I caught an unexpected glance of myself in a security mirror's reflection. In that moment, my brain did an odd thing – it fired off this split-second message: "Hey! You know her! That's a friend of yours!" And I ran forward toward my own reflection with a smile, ready to welcome that girl whose name I had lost but whose face was so familiar. In a flash instant of course, I realised my mistake and laughed in embarrassment at my almost doglike confusion over how a mirror works. But for some reason that incident comes to mind again... Never forget that once upon a time, in an unguarded moment, you recognized yourself as a FRIEND."

Do you have a best friend? I have known mine since I was eleven years old. If I really need her and I concentrate hard enough, I can see her beautiful face and hear her voice in my head. She is hugely compassionate and also has an absolutely wicked sense of humour and – as it has been over 40 years now – I feel like I can hear her in my head during difficult times. This does not negate the real her and, I'm glad to say, she still often surprises me with her wonderful comments and brilliant advice. But, when a shame hole starts to try to drag me into its orbit, I know she would say, 'Nah… I wouldn't go there if I were you', and she'd be right.

Often when my clients are giving themselves a really hard time. I will say … "Hey 'Sarah' - just stop for a moment please – the person you're taking chunks out of is a good friend of mine. Could you stop beating her up please? You wouldn't treat someone else the way you treat yourself."

It always pulls their NoJo in and they are able to see they would not treat another person like they are treating themselves. Being criticised and berated does not help others to be their best and change what they want to change, so why would it work for you?

How would you treat yourself differently if you make a commitment to treat yourself like you do your best friend? What would you say or do? Reflect on your thoughts in your journal.

How To Deal With Comparison: Your Life Is Not A Social Media Highlight Reel

Highlight reels are made up of the moments in our lives where the outfit looks good, the meal turns out right, a family gets together and they all enjoy each other's company. But, of course, the reel shuts off long before any arguments could begin. It's a string of moments we photograph, and, having deleted the photos where we are accidentally pulling stupid faces, share with the world on social media. What's not seen are all the deleted happenings: the outfits we hated, the burnt meal still smoking on your kitchen counter, the family argument, or the end of the wedding where you fall over drunk.

We all know this is true, but then a curious thing happens. You compare your everyday life to other people's highlight reel. This is a human trait of course; it used to be called 'Keeping up with the Joneses'. But social media has amplified it into a life-infiltrating phenomenon.

Highlight reels are only highlights and are definitely not real!

However, if your self-worth holes are active you will tend to forget this fact. Feeling inadequate and inferior, you share more amazing images to your own highlight reel, hoping to make the grade. Other people of course then see your amazing life and are tempted to judge their own.

This habit of comparing ourselves to others and using it to build or diminish our sense of self-worth is not new but social media does seem to have increased it 100-fold. I believe we need to engage with our sense of self with a bit more precision, care, and accuracy.

Comparison with another human being would seem to be a totally natural and human thing to do. I haven't yet met anyone who doesn't compare themselves to other people. Obviously, it would be wonderful if we didn't compare ourselves to others and it would, no doubt, instantly make our lives a lot more peaceful. However, as we don't seem to be able to stop comparing ourselves, we would seem to be in a catch 22 situation.

So instead of scrolling mindlessly through social media, commit to being present to any emotions that come up when you read your friends' posts. Particularly commit to noticing when you are comparing someone's highlights with your 'ordinary' life. Then once you've spotted the comparison, really investigate as to whether that comparison is at a self-worth or a self-esteem level.

How do you know if your comparison is at a self-worth level?
It really hurts!
You get defensive, angry, upset. You push it away or criticise them. Your self-defence mechanisms come right up.

It might only be a tiny pinprick of jealousy at someone's outfit/new car/partner/children/job/holiday/LIFE! But, if you let yourself follow that tiny pinprick and listen to the thoughts powering that emotion, what are they saying? If they lead to feelings of "that person is better than me" or "I am not good enough" then it is undoubtedly getting in at a self-worth level. You have found a self-worth hole. You now know where to focus and what work you need to do next.

You can choose to investigate what is true and not true. You could become your own coach and follow that process, or you can do any of the exercises in this book. Just please do not 'ignore it' or just 'push it away or down'. It has come up because you're ready to heal it!

How do you know if your comparison is at a self-esteem level?
If the tiny pinprick of discontent/jealousy/envy leads you to a sense that there is something in your life that you might want to change. Something in your life isn't quite as you would like it – great! – then you are free to investigate it further. For example, are

you comparing like-for-like?

Remember, highlight reels are highlights, and definitely not real!

If somebody is talking about their perfect job and it looks like it would be perfect for you and you wish you had it, then take a moment to enquire: would you also be willing to take that job on a really terrible day? It is very unlikely that there is going to be a social media post about that day! If that person's perfect job has an amazing salary that you want, take a moment to remember the time, effort, stress, qualifications, travel, hard work, and sacrifice that that salary most likely represents. Do you want the whole thing, not just the honeymoon period? If the answer is 'no' you can let the thoughts of comparison go as you are not comparing like-for-like.

However, if it is a 'yes' and you want all those things, then your inner self may be demonstrating to you that your job is no longer right for you and you need a new challenge, a new focus, or perhaps a completely new job.

Sally's Story

Sally had been coaching with me for six months. She loved her job and believed she wanted promotion to the next level and yet couldn't quite seem to achieve it. During one session she shared with me some prohibited and disallowed bad feelings of jealousy and envy when noticing her friends' Facebook posts of their children. She had a partner that she loved but he also had a very high-powered job and children were not in his near future.

Once Sally had allowed herself to feel these feelings, she courageously followed them. She worked at healing the self-worth holes that were telling her that she was worth less than her friends because she didn't have children. This was deep work and required much commitment. However, as the months went on and her self-worth became more stable, she was more able to observe that the comparison she was still making was demonstrating the feeling from her deepest inner self that she wanted a child.

Sally's journey was not easy or quick, but she now has a baby boy and is a very proud and capable single mum. Contrary to popular belief, we don't get everything we want in this world and sometimes allowing yourself to observe other possibilities, with your self-worth intact, can show you that perhaps your jealousy is demonstrating where you have not honoured your deepest wishes yet.

Sally is the happiest I have ever known her, with a very happy, well cared for and balanced little boy. And she decided that she didn't want that promotion, or at least, not for a few years yet.

Reflect on what you have just read in your journal. Where and how are you comparing your life with someone else's highlights? What is this telling you about your own self-worth holes?

One Minute Exercise: Just Stop And Breathe

STOP. Feel your feet on the floor (or bum on the chair) and let the floor (or chair) take your weight.

As you relax and breathe, consider your unique SELF from the ground up; your feet, legs, hips, torso, arms, chest, neck and head. Feel into your YOU-NESS. The fact you are individual and unique.

Remember what your current record is at being you?
Answer... 100%. Well done!
Although this exercise takes under a minute, it can be extended for as long as you feel able!

Forgiveness And Self-Worth

Forgiveness is a huge topic! There are so many wonderful books on it and growing all the time. But I will note that if forgiveness comes from an esteem level rather than a worth level then it is flawed, and I believe won't achieve the peace that forgiveness from a worth level can bring. Forgiveness from the self-esteem level can quickly become superior, condescending and even judgemental. I would go so far as to say that forgiveness isn't really forgiveness at all if it doesn't acknowledge the other person's worth as a human being as distinct from their actions.

Are there things that you haven't forgiven others for? It's worth noting down in your journal, anything that comes to mind, however small, where you believe that you're still holding a grudge. Dig out anything that you haven't truly forgiven, even from your school days.

Not forgiving someone means that you have given that person power over your emotions. That will be affecting you and could be feeding a self-worth hole. You are literally carrying with you heavy emotions from the past, which require a lot of emotional energy to keep them contained even if you've got a really good set of psychological storage boxes! That means you're losing your energy because of the other person's behaviour, possibly not forgiving yourself and taking chunks out of your self-worth. Is that okay with you?

"Resentment is like drinking poison and then waiting for the other person to die," Carrie Fisher (in her book The Best Awful: A Novel 2003).

If you haven't forgiven other people, it can be very hard to forgive yourself.

"Forgive others, not because they deserve forgiveness, but because you deserve peace,"
Mel Robbins

There are so many incredible feats of forgiveness that can truly inspire us so that we can forgive the people we need to. If I am struggling to forgive, I remember the story of the parents of Amy

Biehl who forgave the men who murdered their daughter. Amy, an American anti-apartheid activist, was murdered in Cape Town in 1993. The men were pardoned during Nelson Mandela's Truth and Reconciliation Commission. It always has me in tears of wonder, admiration and gratitude.

Forgiveness is an attribute of the strong. There is nothing weak about forgiveness. To really understand it is complex and to actually do it is tough, real work. I do not believe it is about people not being accountable for their actions, or the consequences thereof. being 'let off'. It is an act of fierce love and uncompromising compassion.

Of course, forgiving others will not add anything to your sense of inner peace unless you have deeply forgiven yourself. And this means truly forgiving yourself, not because you did nothing wrong (this may, or may not be true, only you will know), but because it was your actions, not your worth. You are perfect at your worth level. Forgive yourself for being you!

Remember that to truly heal your self-worth holes you must clear all the toxic shame. Healthy shame is not pleasant, but it reminds us we are flawed human beings and stops us becoming overly self-centred. Toxic shame stops us becoming ourselves.

A Final Exercise: Deepening Your Sense Of Self-Worth By Celebrating You!

When did you last truly celebrate YOU! Celebrate that you are here and celebrate that you are you!

Here's some ideas:
- Take yourself on a date
- Buy yourself a bunch of flowers for no reason
- Put your favourite track on and dance just with you
- Be creative and make something, anything, just for the act of making a unique thing

- Make time to celebrate with nature – stand barefoot on the Earth. (There are lots of other benefits of this – look up the science about the benefits of grounding)
- Make time to look at the stars to gaze at the sky. You are made of stardust you belong under that sky

My favourite: the 'celebrate me' walk.

I love to do this special walk with the turning of the year. It reminds me that I am part of this earth and cosmos. I have cycles and rhythms, ups and downs. I do a 'celebrate me' walk in spring, summer, autumn and winter. That's only four walks a year – I bet you can fit that in! Don't walk the dog, don't plan the list of jobs you'll do when you get back, don't even listen to a podcast. Focus on your feet taking each step and celebrate yourself being on the Earth. Feel your connection and belonging to the earth and sky.

Notice, really notice, the 'being' qualities of the world around you:
- The abundance and lushness of summer
- The let go and die back of autumn
- The bareness and stillness of winter
- The passion and generosity of the bursting spring

Notice your senses and celebrate each one. Let your heart connect with all of it and know that you are here, you are worthy, and you are you – that is enough. Take a moment to breathe. Feel that worthiness flood through your body. Feel a deep appreciation for you just as you are without doing anything, just a human-being.

As you return home, renew your commitment that any actions you do come from a deep reverence for yourself. Acknowledge your physical, emotional, mental, and big picture levels of being. Breathe and know you have worth.

"You are a child of the universe, no less than the trees and the stars; you have a right to be here." Desiderata.

A GIFT FOR YOU!
FREE ACCESS TO THE
HOW TO BE BRAVE
ONLINE COURSE:

There are more tips and exercises on Indigo Brave's website. As you have bought this book, you also get free access to the How to be Brave online course here:

www.indigobrave.com

SOME FINAL THOUGHTS

Thank you for reading my book. I hope you are inspired to join in my campaign to the Oxford English Dictionary to change those definitions of self-worth and self-esteem so that we can change the narrative for our babies, children, teenagers, apprentices, workers, colleagues, and parents. We need to let everyone know that to feel better in their own skin they must connect with their innate attributes as a human being, not work harder, achieve more and do more.

If you're breathing, you have worth.

Do not confuse your 'value' to another person, a system, an organisation or a community with your 'worth'. You are not a thing – and you are definitely not a resource! It is not possible to assign a value to your 'you-ness' that is a result of the concept of money and counting and numbers.

You don't have to believe in a creator or God or 'the divine' to see that you are infinitely complex and way more than your actions. You don't have to prove your worth. In fact, you can't. Only you can know it and you decide it, not others. Your worth is in your being-ness, the fact that you are here.

You can be present to yourself and others and that is enough. If you can be, you have worth. You are not a human-doing; you are a human-being.

The more you feel your innate, unassailable worth, the more your cup fills from the inside and you naturally want to share that with others, your family, your community, your workplace, from a feeling of overflowing connection and desire to give of yourself.

If you are rejected, you get something wrong or you make a bad mistake, and you are in touch with that intrinsic sense of worth, you can take it. Your resilience is strong. You can hold yourself accountable; because this is just something you have done; it is not who you are. And you have qualities that you are well acquainted with that can help you to put this right. You are then magically free from the co-dependence that plagues our modern relationships.

You are free of judgement or rejection of another. As you know your worth, so their judgements must be either about things you have done or misguided in some way. What they think of you is not really your business. And you are also, therefore, magically free from the modern-day scourge of narcissism – for you love the real you! Not the image of you projected in 'your highlight reel' on social media!

You are real, flawed, imperfectly perfect. You. Any amount of self-development is for just that – development. Growth and evolution are beautiful, but there is nothing to 'fix' in who you are – that's you. You can fix and change what you *do* as much as you like – that's your esteem. I hope with all my heart you are already making insights to where these two essentially different concepts are 'coagulated' and mixed up in your life, because it can literally be life changing when you can.

The exercises you have embarked on here are the start of a journey into yourself. It is a good start, but it is only the start. Like any good journey it will show you some things that you did not expect as well as taking you in a direction you chose. You may well discover there is a lot more to you than you expected, perhaps even more dimensions in which your consciousness, your 'self' can exist and can become aware of itself. Perhaps you will join the ever-growing movement of human beings experiencing something beyond their physical, rational existence, and have a personal experience of something transcendent, out of body, even spiritual. If this happens, wonderful. We are with you. We have supported clients through these kinds of experiences too. We look forward to hearing about it :) But, the point of this book is there is no need for that.

You are enough exactly as you are, and I sincerely hope this book gives you a reason to believe that, perhaps more than you have ever believed it. You are you. You are of worth. End of story. Now, write yourself a new one.

POSTSCRIPT

How Working With The Self Model™ Helped Me Write This Book

The process of getting this book published has brought me right up against my old struggles once again.

"Who am I to write a book?! No-one will be interested! Good grief, you are simply not clever enough! What makes you think your ideas are new?"

I am used to those voices. I have had them all my life. I have tried for many years to silence them, but it never works for long. I know if they are criticising my self-worth, then they're wrong, instantly, no question, easy. I have worked hard at that. That cannot be true, because my worth just is. I can differentiate between a voice that is my old self-worth holes (wired-in neural networks) firing off in my brain. That voice tells infinite variations on the theme that I am not good enough and I must fix that by doing more, and better, and quickly. Thank you for sharing, I tell the voice, but that is not true. I stop and I do some self-worth work.

But what if the voices I can hear are criticising at a 'doing' level (like writing a book!)?

I have learnt I can treat them as a friend. What if they are trying to help me? Keep me safe? Save me from disappointment, from the 'hell' of failure? I have learnt to listen to them and enquire into them; to be curious and to explore if they are true?

When the voices came up about this book, and boy did they come up a plenty, I used my *Be your own coach* tool and started to enquire. Checking my self-worth was firmly in place and my membrane was strong, I asked:

"OK voice, thank you for sharing that my book is rubbish. I certainly wouldn't want to go to all this effort if it was rubbish, so let's enquire and do some reality testing."

I invited the voice to let rip with all her fears and I scribbled them down:

"You're showing off if you write a book – it's an ego trip.
No-one will read it or be interested.
It will be embarrassing.
You are simply not clever enough!
The model isn't useful or important enough to warrant a book.
What makes you think your ideas are new?"

With some brave enquiry, it was clear that I could simply not know that they were true.

"Thank you for sharing. I know these fears are not true because I feel/ have experienced /really know:

I can write a sentence; therefore, I can technically write a book.
This model has really helped people to change their lives.
Many clients have asked me to write it, so they want it at least!
Yes, it will probably be very embarrassing at moments, but that is ok, I can process that."

But there was one fear that I couldn't be sure wasn't valid:

> Are the ideas new?
> Has it been done before?
> Am I just rehashing old ideas?

The voices were loud. I started to worry. What if the voices are right and it is just too simple, and everybody already knows this?

If the voices are too persistent for you to hold and discern whether they are true, or just attempts to stop you doing something right out of your comfort zone, I ask for help. So, with my self-worth membrane as firmly intact as I could manage, I called one of my cleverest friends who happens to be a psychologist. I asked if I could buy her lunch and ask a work question.

I was nervous. I'd heard about a guy who had discovered a place on the body that had a different electrical charge to other places. Nobel Prize here we come! He had spent years of study completing his PhD, mapping all the spots on the body with this different charge. He thought he was changing the world. When he'd finished his PhD, he'd actually just mapped out the Acupuncture map. This wisdom has been known for approximately 3,000 – 5,000 years, and even in written down form since 100 BC. Not so new.

So, I decided to give my inner voices a reality check. Through my love of Improv Comedy, I had met Serena Simmons (CPsychol BSc, BA, MSc), a brilliant psychology lecturer, so asked her for some time.

I explained the model and asked if I was re-hashing an old idea. "Absolutely not", she said. "I have never heard it before. It makes perfect sense to me and I think I might be able to use it this afternoon! Stop the voices which want to keep you small and safe and write that book."

OK, that was clear. I just need to get over the fear of other people's criticism, the fear inside me of getting it wrong and feeling exposed and shamed!

She asked me a great question; "Why are you writing the book in the first place?".

"Well, I want this shift in thinking to reach more people than Indigo Brave can reach by coaching and workshops. Also, clients have repeatedly asked me for a book to support them to reflect on what this shift in their thinking might look like, helping them to understand the subtleties, the depths of this work."

"So, the only question you have to ask yourself is: Is the motivation to write the book stronger than the fears of criticism it might bring," said Serena.

That made perfect sense to me. It has taken me 10 years to write this book! Sure, I have been busy trying to run a business, raise the children, survive the fire, and build our eco-home. But that's not really it. I have met plenty of 'book people' who have encouraged me, they have been supportive and even reported back to me that the model was of real value and had helped them in their lives.

A client from America was training with me in the UK; he asked where he could read more about The SELF Model™. I knew he wouldn't find anything.

Another client wanted to use the model with his teenage son who was incredibly bright but struggling to connect and communicate. He knew the model inside out, but he was finding it hard to explain because his son kept saying, "that's not what I have been taught at school." He even went and looked it up in the dictionary. "You're wrong Dad, everyone says they are the same."

This is what made me want to get the book finished this time.

The model is Indigo Brave's, and it was up to us to spread the word. I needed to write that book!

All I had to do was to face my fears that it might be rubbish; even if I try my hardest and pour in blood, sweat and tears, I still might hate it when I've written it. Can I accept that and get on with it? Believe me, it's a tough one! If I hate this book, then it will certainly make my self-esteem plummet, and can I really be OK with that? Well, if my desire to help people is stronger than the desire not to have to feel the self-esteem low of hating what I had written, then yes, I can be OK with that!

I was finding some time to write and finishing chapters here and there when I met the wonderful book doula, Rebecca. She loved the idea and got it straight away. She got in touch the next day and let me know she thought I should write the book and she believed she could help me.

She encouraged me to just write and write and write. She said it was fine that I had no idea what the book might be like when it was finished, put aside judgement or criticism, just write. Yup, I hated the first version, and the second, the third was really bad, and it may well have just stayed there on my laptop, with all the other times I had started, if it wasn't for that question echoing in my head:

"Which is going to win; your desire to help people or your desire to stay safe?"

Right! It had taken a house fire for me to let go of perfectionism and record Agent LaLa's first CD, and I knew I did not want another of those! Could I forgive myself for daring to write a book when I knew I was not as good as all the amazing writers I so admire, and just let this book be 'good enough'.

Yes, I could. When I was so fed up with staring at my screen, I would use the motivation of the look on someone's face when they really get the model. When I was wrestling with my inability to make a sentence say what I wanted to say, I remembered the experience of someone getting that they are genuinely OK, whatever they have done.

And I kept remembering that it will only be my esteem which will take a beating if I hate it. And I did hate it! And my esteem did take a beating. But, if you're reading this, which must at least be version five, then my drive to get this information to as many people as possible and Rebecca's determination to finally get this book over the line, got us there.

The irony that writing my book meant I had to take another dive into the truth that "It's not about self-esteem, self-worth is the key to success", did not escape me. I was afforded yet another opportunity to dig deep and see where I could do some more mending of those self-worth holes.

WANT MORE FROM INDIGO BRAVE?

Indigo Brave's mission is to inspire and facilitate your growth and success, so that, together, we can create a more profitable, sustainable, and joyful world.

The SELF Model™ is the basis of our methodology. We have continued to build on that and now have other, equally effective models and methods which allow you to create the change you want. (Hopefully, I will write those books too… eventually!)

Further details can be found at Indigobrave.com and teachable.indigobrave.com

Can Indigo Brave Help you? We work with individuals and teams in Blue Chip companies, SMEs, charities and in education. We are a triple bottom line business, as we were when we set up in 1996. This means that we audit ourselves on People, Planet and Profit.

We offer our work at subsidised rates for young people, charities, and the education sector.

We are values driven. We will always make sure our work is available to anyone who wants it! We run programmes to support people with long-term mental health histories and vulnerable teenagers as well as working with C-suite executives, senior leaders, and leaders of the future through our apprentice programmes.

Future Leaders

Young people are the future, and we want to support them to be their best, so they can show us the way! We work with apprentices, creating bespoke programmes to support them to excel in all the skills they will need in the workplace.

The SELF Camps

Sustainable, Emotionally intelligent Learning for the Future (SELF) is a three-day camping experience taking 13-year-old girls into nature with no makeup, no mirrors and no phones! It is based in Nottinghamshire but has ambitions to be national, open to all young women and is a truly transformational journey of self-discovery. (SELF Camps for young men are planned for summer 2024.)

Quantum Success For Women Execs

For women who wish to go further in their career without compromising their home/family life or their health. Using principles from quantum physics and the latest neuroscience research, QSWE could be the tool you need to take you as far as you want to go in all areas of your life.

Quantum Success For Men Execs

Where is the healthy masculine heading in our society? Is there a place for men to be men anymore? Can a male executive embrace his 'feminine side', his sensitivity, his vulnerability, his softness, and his receptivity and still be successful in his career, and at being a man? Yes! This course teaches you how to be authentically you and a high performing exec and step into your real, raw masculine power as well!

One-To-One Coaching

Purpose, authenticity, and deep embodiment to your physical, emotional, mental, and big picture self. No matter what walk of life you are in, our methods allow you to discover how to succeed by becoming more of who you really are. We support you to understand how to peel off the layers of conditioning that aren't you.

Create A C-Change (Improving Business Through Culture Enhancement)

Of course, you are perfecting your company's strategy, ensuring it drives your direction, growth, sales and profit, and you probably have clear and well-thought through values, but is this enough? Is the dominant culture of your business helping or hindering your strategy? Your culture is what actually happens in your business every day. It's the habits and behaviours, the relationships and the spaces between people that are there, day-in day-out. It is not a laminated sheet on the wall, it's the 'identity' of your business.

Your culture is the life blood of your business. It is what drives it forward to success and the reason people stay. Aligning culture and strategy through your values contributes significantly to your bottom line and supports the development and wellbeing of your people.

ACKNOWLEDGEMENTS

Firstly, I want to acknowledge my Book Doula, Rebecca Brittain, LuBabebooks.co.uk. Clients have been asking me if I could write more about The SELF Model™ in a book for over 10 years. I have had many goes at it since then! I honestly believe it would never have happened without you, Becca. You used the model from the beginning and believed it would make a really good book. Your encouragement, determination, patience, and insistence that this book should happen have been absolutely key to me getting this book over the line. Thank you for helping make a book that is good enough!

Our first clients! You showed us the way. Thank you.

All our clients! Everyone who has coached with me, done a workshop, purchased a workshop or series for their company, brought us in to work with their team, bought a video, seen a play/performance, bought a CD, or engaged with Indigo Brave in any way, shape or form. Thank you! It is impossible to offer this work if no-one wants to listen and the trust you have shown us in humbling. I am so very grateful.

My colleagues, Harinda Ghatora and Nicolas David Ngan, for invaluable help with the title and cover and for continuous encouragement and belief, and Serena Simmons, for your insistence that The SELF Model™ offered value and insight and should be out in the world; thank you for believing in me when I wobbled!

To my amazing family and my fabulous sisters! Thank you for putting up with me and my peculiar ways for so long now. Thank you from the bottom of my heart for always being there and being you! A huge thank you to my sister Lucy for brilliant proofreading and keeping me writing when I wanted to burn the whole thing.

My friends! Oh, my friends. I am not going to name you because it seems a tad garish – you know who you are. And you particularly know exactly who you are (I bow in gratitude). You have saved my life. You have put me back together again and again. You have enriched my life beyond words. What adventures and fabulous times we have had, and I have loved it. More please! You have shown up and propped up and shut me up and I simply adore you. Between me and insanity stand my friends. Thank you.

My husband Mathew, thank you for your steadfast belief in the need for this book to be written and the constant encouragement to just get on with it and write the thing. And of course, to Luke and Esmée, our children. You are absolute miracles of people. I am so immensely grateful to you for being here. Our family has weathered the ups and downs and catastrophic storms, and I couldn't be more in awe of how we have done it, together! You are the most creative, authentic, hilarious, loving, outrageous, talented, and amazing people I know. Thank you for putting up with me: my intensity, planning, freak outs, wounds, failures, and insecurities. I love you.

And thank you to you, dear reader. If you have enjoyed this book, please help spread the word and leave an Amazon review.

Thank you.

ABOUT THE AUTHOR

Laila-Elizabeth Risdon

Laila-Elizabeth Risdon BA (Hons) MA, is one of the founders of the award-winning, triple bottom line company, Indigo Brave Group Ltd. Her coaching and workshops have helped over 20,000 people create real and lasting changes in their lives, through Indigo Brave's proprietary methodology, which includes The SELF Model™. Laila and the Indigo Brave team support business leaders, senior teams, and future leaders in the corporate, Education and Third sectors; leaders who wish to create success through developing a more collaborative, emotionally intelligent, and high-performance culture. Laila also runs Indigo Brave Social Enterprise, working with vulnerable adults and teens, supporting improved wellbeing and mental health. She is married with two children and lives in a passive house on a smallholding, as part of a sustainable, eco-project. She loves to spend time on the smallholding, tending the veg plots, polytunnels, bees, sheep, and chickens, using biodynamic and permaculture methods. She also enjoys camping, adventures and walking her dogs! She loves to sing and is a member of two choirs, as well as writing and performing with her band, Agent LaLa. A student of Qi Gong, Tai Ji, Five Rhythms dance, Improv Comedy, cold water swimming, singing, regenerative agriculture, music, and many forms of meditation, increasing her presence and deepening her level of consciousness continues to be her passion. She is thrilled to be able to support as many people as possible to live more connected, empowered, joyful, sustainable, and successful lives.

Printed in Great Britain
by Amazon